THE COMPLETE GUIDE TO
GOLF

ON CAPE COD, NANTUCKET AND MARTHA'S VINEYARD

To
Diane, Jon-Michael, and Tina,
members of my most precious foursome

THE COMPLETE GUIDE TO
GOLF

ON CAPE COD, NANTUCKET AND MARTHA'S VINEYARD

BY PAUL HARBER

THE PENINSULA PRESS
CAPE COD

Text copyright ©1993 by Paul Harber.
Cover design by Betsy Roscoe Morin.
Cover watercolor by David P. Wallis.

Published by
The Peninsula Press · Post Office Box 644 · Cape Cod 02670 USA
Donald W. Davidson
Publisher

All rights reserved.
No part of this publication may be reproduced,
stored in a retrieval system, or transmitted in any form or by any means
— electronic, mechanical, photocopying, recording, or otherwise —
without prior written permission of the publisher.
Native Guide™ is a trademark of The Peninsula Press.

First published in 1994 by The Peninsula Press.

Library of Congress Catalog Card Number: 93-087226
Harber, Paul.
  The Complete Guide to Golf on Cape Cod, Nantucket & Martha's Vineyard
  The Peninsula Press, ©1994.
  Includes index, bibliography, and illustrations.
  ISBN 1-883684-02-1
  1. Cape Cod, Nantucket & Martha's Vineyard -- Golf.
  2. Cape Cod, Nantucket & Martha's Vineyard -- History and recreation.
  3. Cape Cod, Nantucket & Martha's Vineyard -- Geography and geology.

First edition
Manufactured on Cape Cod in the United States of America
2 3 4 5 6 7 8 9 / 02 01 00 99 98 97 96 95 94

Contents

Preface
                                                    Page 11

The Growth of Golf
                                                    Page 13

SECTION I:
   The History of Golf on Cape Cod, Nantucket & Martha's Vineyard

Chapter 1: Golf in This Kingdom
                                                    Page 17

Chapter 2: The Basic Layout
                                                    Page 22

Chapter 3: A Vanishing Breed
                                                    Page 29

Chapter 4: One Brief Shining Moment
                                                    Page 36

Chapter 5: Good Day at Blue Rock
                                                    Page 41

Chapter 6: The New Beginning
                                                    Page 47

Chapter 7: The Once & Future Kingdom
                                                    Page 52

SECTION II:

A list of Native Guides to the Golf Courses on Cape Cod, Nantucket & Martha's Vineyard

COURSE, *Site*/Telephone (Area Code 508)				
Holes	Par	Yards	Tee time policy	

BALLYMEADE, *N. Falmouth*/540-4005
 18 holes par 72 6,928 yds -------- (Semi-private)
 Page 58

BASS RIVER, *S. Yarmouth*/398-9079
 18 holes par 72 5,702 yds 4 days (Town-owned)
 Page 60

BAYBERRY HILLS, *W. Yarmouth*/394-5597
 18 holes par 72 6,067 yds 4 days (Town-owned)
 Page 62

BAY POINTE, *Wareham*/759-8802
 18 holes par 71 6,201 yds 7 days (Daily fee)
 Page 64

BLUE ROCK, *S. Yarmouth*/398-9295
 18 holes par 54 2,746 yds 7 days (Daily fee)
 Page 66

CAPE COD, *N. Falmouth*/563-9842
 18 holes par 71 6,404 yds 7 days (Daily fee)
 Page 68

CAPTAINS, *Brewster*/896-5100
 18 holes par 72 6,170 yds 2 days* (Town-owned)
 Page 70

CHEQUESSETT, *Wellfleet*/349-3704
 9 holes par 35 2,561 yds 1 day (Semi-private)
 Page 72

COTUIT HIGHGROUND, *Cotuit*/428-9863
 9 holes par 28 2,325 yds 1 day (Daily fee)
 Page 74

CRANBERRY VALLEY, *Harwich*/430-7560
 18 holes par 72 6,296 yds 2 days* (Town-owned)
 Page 76

CUMMAQUID, *Yarmouthport*/362-2022
 18 holes par 71 6,302 yds -------- (Private)
 Page 78

• 6 •

DENNIS HIGHLANDS, *Dennis* /385-8347
    18 holes   par 71   6,464 yds   4 days* (Town-owned)
    Page 80

DENNIS PINES, *Dennis*/385-8698
    18 holes   par 72   7,029 yds   4 days* (Town-owned)
    Page 82

EASTWARD HO! *Chathamport*/945-0620
    18 holes   par 72   6,215 yds   -------- (Private)
    Page 84

EDGARTOWN, *Edgartown/Martha's Vineyard*/627-5343
    9 holes   par 36   2,845 yds   -------- (Private)
    Page 86

FALMOUTH, *E. Falmouth*/548-3211
    18 holes   par 72   6,227 yds   7 days (Daily fee)
    Page 88

FARM NECK, *Oak Bluffs/Martha's Vineyard*/693-3057
    18 holes   par 72   6,330 yds   2 days (Semi-private)
    Page 90

HARWICHPORT, *Harwich Port*/432-0250
    9 holes   par 34   2,538 yds   None (Daily fee)
    Page 92

HIGHLAND LINKS, *N. Truro*/487-9201
    9 holes   par 36   2,789 yds   1 week (Daily fee)
    Page 94

HOLLY RIDGE, *S. Sandwich*/428-5577
    18 holes   par 54   2,952 yds   1 day (Daily fee)
    Page 96

HYANNIS, *Hyannis*/362-2606
    18 holes   par 71   6,400 yds   1 month (Daily fee)
    Page 98

HYANNISPORT, *Hyannisport*/775-2978
    18 holes   par 71   6,260 yds   -------- (Private)
    Page 100

KINGS WAY, *Yarmouthport*/362-8820
    18 holes   par 59   4,023 yds   3 days (Semi-private)
    Page 102

KITTANSETT, *Marion*/748-0192
    18 holes   par 71   6,640 yds   -------- (Private)
    Page 104

LITTLE HARBOR, *Wareham*/295-2617
    18 holes   par 56   3,038 yds   3 days   (Daily fee)
        Page 106

LITTLE MARION, *Marion*/748-0199
    9 holes   par 34   2,695 yds   --------   (Daily fee)
        Page 108

MIACOMET, *Nantucket*/228-9764
    9 holes   par 37   3,337 yds   1 week   (Daily fee)
        Page 110

MINK MEADOWS, *Vineyard Haven/Martha's Vineyard*/693-0600
    9 holes   par 35   3,002 yds   1 day   (Daily fee)
        Page 112

NEW SEABURY (Blue), *Mashpee*/477-9400
    18 holes   par 72   7,200 yds   1 day   (Semi-private)
        Page 114

NEW SEABURY (Green), *Mashpee*/477-9400
    18 holes   par 70   5,939 yds   1 day   (Semi-private)
        Page 115

OCEAN EDGE, *Brewster*/896-5911
    18 holes   par 72   6,665 yds   1 day   (Semi-private)
        Page 116

OLDE BARNSTABLE FAIRGROUNDS, *Marstons Mills*/420-1141
    18 holes   par 71   6,500 yds   2 days   (Town-owned)
        Page 118

OTIS, *Bourne*/968-6453
    9 holes   par 36   3,307 yds   --------   (Military)
        Page 120

OYSTER HARBORS, *Osterville*/428-9881
    18 holes   par 72   6,687 yds   --------   (Private)
        Page 122

PAUL HARNEY, *N. Falmouth*/563-3454
    18 holes   par 59   3,330 yds   None   (Daily fee)
        Page 124

PLYMOUTH, *Plymouth*/746-0476
    18 holes   par 69   6,164 yds   1 day   (Semi-private)
        Page 126

POCASSET, *Pocasset*/563-7171
    18 holes   par 72   6,225 yds   --------   (Private)
        Page 128

QUASHNET VALLEY, *Mashpee*/477-4412
 18 holes par 72 6,360 yds 1 week (Semi-private)
                    Page 130

RIDGE CLUB, *S. Sandwich*/428-6800
 18 holes par 71 6,282 yds -------- (Private)
                    Page 132

ROUND HILL, *Sandwich*/888-3384
 18 holes par 71 6,157 yds 1 week (Daily fee)
                    Page 134

SANKATY HEAD, *Siasconset*/257-6655
 18 holes par 72 6,465 yds -------- (Private)
                    Page 136

SEASIDE LINKS, *Chatham*/945-4774
 9 holes par 34 2,325 yds None (Town-owned)
                    Page 138

SIASCONSET, *Siasconset*/257-6596
 9 holes par 35 2,543 yds None (Daily fee)
                    Page 140

SQUIRREL RUN, *Plymouth*/746-9588
 18 holes par 58 2,765 yds 1 week (Daily fee)
                    Page 142

TARA WOODS, *Hyannis*/775-7775
 18 holes par 54 2,621 yds 2 days (Daily fee)
                    Page 144

WHITE CLIFFS, *Cedarville*/888-7800
 18 holes par 62 3,909 yds -------- (Private)
                    Page 146

WIANNO, *Osterville*/428-9840
 18 holes par 70 5,900 yds -------- (Private)
                    Page 148

WILLOWBEND, *Mashpee*/477-8888
 18 holes par 71 6,785 yds -------- (Private)
                    Page 150

WOODBRIAR, *Falmouth*/540-1600
 9 holes par 27 1,410 yds None (Daily fee)
                    Page 152

WOODS HOLE, *Falmouth*/548-2932
 18 holes par 71 6,117 yds -------- (Private)
                    Page 154

"The Game of Golf" by L.C. Hall
    from *CAPE COD Magazine* (April, 1923)

Page 156

Index

Bibliography

Acknowledgments

* Asterisk in *Tee time policy* column indicates that times can be reserved one year in advance if prepaid.

Preface

Little did our forefathers realize what they started when they used their wooden-shafted clubs to hit a feathery ball across an open field in the farmlands of Cummaquid or on the high lands of North Truro.

There were no photographers on hand to record the momentous beginning. There were no newspaper reporters nearby to summarize the earliest rounds. And there was no more passion toward this particular game than there was toward any game of horseshoes or even croquet. In those days, golf was just another diversion for those who came to visit in the summer.

A century later, though, golf on Cape Cod, Nantucket & Martha's Vineyard has become a big business, and only one other region in all of America has more golf courses per capita than does the Cape & Islands: South Carolina's Myrtle Beach. Meanwhile, right here there are some forty-nine places where you can play golf, fifty courses in all. That translates into seven hundred and ninety-two tees, fairways and greens to accommodate those who have developed a passion for this game, a passion that is far greater than that displayed for any other game in America.

With that in mind, I present this book not as *the* definitive history of golf on Cape Cod, Nantucket & Martha's Vineyard, but as both a comprehensive history to give you a greater sense of the game on the Cape & Islands, as well as a guide to provide you with some direction in selecting those courses in this area that you might wish to play.

Paul Harber
January, 1994

PAUL HARBER has been a member of the *Boston Globe* sports staff since 1979, where he has covered the New England golf scene since 1984. His writings have also appeared in *Golf World*, as well as the *Massachusetts Golfer*, and he appears regularly on the syndicated television program *Golf New England*.

When he isn't pecking away on his home computer or covering a tournament, Paul can often be found at his home course, Thorny Lea Golf Club in Brockton. There he is either playing the boys in a $5 Nassau, or else dueling his wife, Diane, in a pressure-packed "Slave-of-the-Day Match," wherein the loser must wash the dishes, clean the house, and relinquish all rights whatsoever to the television remote control.

Though we do not know for certain, perhaps his luck in those matches with his spouse accounts for the fact that he does not spend a great deal of time watching TV. In fact, during the ten years that Paul has been living with his golf addiction, he has traipsed around more than 250 courses, compiling over 2,500 rounds and taking an incalculable number of strokes. And because his home is less than an hour's drive from the Sagamore and Bourne bridges, he has crossed the Cape Cod Canal countless times in relentless pursuit of that elusive birdie.

Perhaps when you play these courses for yourself, you might find Paul just a chipshot away. If so, wish him the same luck he hopes this book might bring to you.

The Growth of Golf

1892:	Highland Links, *North Truro*
1893:	Seapuit, *Osterville*
1894:	Siasconset, *Nantucket*
1895:	Cummaquid, *Barnstable*
1896:	Nantucket Links, *Nantucket*
	Oak Bluffs, *Oak Bluffs/Martha's Vineyard*
1898:	Woods Hole, *Woods Hole*
1900:	Bass River, *South Yarmouth*
1906:	Marion, *Marion*
1908:	Hyannisport Club, *Hyannisport*
	Plymouth, *Plymouth*
1914:	Chatham Bars Inn, *Chatham*
c.1915:	Menauhant, *Falmouth*
	Ben Lomond, *Sagamore*
	Cedar Bank, *Eastham*
1916:	The Wianno Club, *Osterville*
	Pocasset, *Pocasset*
1918:	Harwichport, *Harwich Port*
1922:	Eastward Ho!, *Chathamport*
c.1920s:	Tupancy, *Nantucket*
	Santuit, *Mashpee*
1923:	Sankaty Head, *Siasconset*
	The Kittansett Club, *Marion*
1927:	Oyster Harbors, *Osterville*
	Edgartown, *Edgartown/Martha's Vineyard*
1929:	Coonamesset, *North Falmouth*

	Cotuit Highground, *Cotuit*
	Chequessett, *Wellfleet*
1936:	Mink Meadows, *Vineyard Haven/MV*
c.1950s:	Treadway, *North Falmouth*
1961:	White Cliffs, *Cedarville*
1962:	Blue Rock, *South Yarmouth*
1963:	Little Harbor, *Wareham*
	Miacomet, *Nantucket*
1964:	Otis, *Bourne*
	Falmouth, *East Falmouth*
	Country Club of New Seabury, *Mashpee*
	Clausen's, *North Falmouth*
1965:	Wareham, *Wareham*
	Dennis Pines, *Dennis*
1966:	Holly Ridge, *South Sandwich*
	Fiddler's Green, *Hyannis*
1967:	Ashumuth Valley /Paul Harney's, *Hatchville*
1971:	Round Hill, *East Sandwich*
1974:	Cranberry Valley, *Harwich*
1973:	Iyanough Hills, *Hyannis*
	Grasmere, *Falmouth*
	Brewster Green, *Brewster*
1976:	Farm Neck, *Oak Bluffs/Martha's Vineyard*
	Quashnet Valley, *Mashpee*
1978:	Woodbriar, *Falmouth*
1985:	Dennis Highlands , *Dennis*
	The Captains, *Brewster*
1986:	Brookside, *Bourne*
	White Cliffs Country Club, *Cedarville*
	Ocean Edge, *Brewster*
	Bay Pointe, *Wareham*
1988:	Kings Way, *Yarmouthport*
	Bayberry Hills, *West Yarmouth*
	Willowbend, *Mashpee*
1989:	Ballymeade, *North Falmouth*
	Hyannis, *Hyannis*
	Seaside Links, *Chatham*
1990:	The Ridge Club, *South Sandwich*
1992:	Olde Barnstable Fairgrounds, *Marstons Mills*
	Squirrel Run, *Plymouth*

Section I

Notes

Golf in This Kingdom

The richness of golf on Cape Cod, Nantucket & Martha's Vineyard is more than just the measure of recent growth. It is the legacy of the game's early origins, local origins that hearken back to days more than a hundred years when architects and players alike helped pioneer an interest in golf on this side of the North Atlantic. Despite this significant role in America's sporting heritage, however, the history of golf on the Cape & Islands reflects the ambience of this coastline itself: casual, *very* casual. In fact, few local courses and clubs have any precise history at all of their earliest existence. Often, holes changed from par-3s to par-4s; sometimes, entire layouts grew from 9 to 18 holes; and every now and then, casual courses organized into clubs. All the while, this developing history of golf on Cape Cod, Nantucket & Martha's Vineyard set down a firm foundation for the game's national history, and this local story was even further enhanced by the presence of legitimate legends: from course architects, such as Donald Ross and Herbert Fowler, to champion players, the likes of Bobby Jones and Francis Ouimet. And so, though the historical records might sometimes be lacking, the historical significance of golf on Cape Cod, Nantucket & Martha's Vineyard remains rich with the lore of the game itself.

Specifics aside for the moment, it is safe to assume that

someone probably hit a golf ball in Sandwich or Eastham, in Barnstable or Chatham sometime before 1890; however, two groups continue to vie for certain bragging rights that date back a century or so. One group belongs to the Highland Golf Links (1892) in North Truro; the other, to Cummaquid Golf Club (1895) in Yarmouthport.

Even then, there are folks in Osterville who to this day maintain that Seapuit Golf Club (1893) deserves some place between them both as the second oldest club on Cape Cod, Nantucket & Martha's Vineyard; however, Seapuit has now been gone for more years than it ever existed. Thus, if Highland Golf Links can claim to be the oldest *course* on the Cape & Islands, then Cummaquid can claim to being the oldest *club*. What had begun as informal sport on the pastured lands of Henry Thacher and Dr. Gorham Bacon in Yarmouth Port and Barnstable in 1893, became a formal organization in 1895. And often it has been associated with the oldest golf club in America, St. Andrews (1888) in Yonkers, New York, that was organized by a Scotsman named John Reed. Reed often spent his summers in Hyannisport, and his sons played now and then at Cummaquid before the emergence of The Hyannisport Club.

Meanwhile, on the island of Nantucket, one golf club had emerged at Siasconset (1894), at a time when the Nantucket Golf Links was being designed by the game's premier architect, Donald Ross. That course would open in 1896, the same year that players at Oak Bluffs Country Club would formally introduce golf to the island of Martha's Vineyard. Add to that circuit the course at Woods Hole (1898), and the number of golf courses on Cape Cod, Nantucket & Martha's Vineyard had grown in less than a decade to at least seven, with others soon to follow.

As the old century turned into the new, golf seemingly spread with a passion throughout the greater Cape & Islands. Courses were opening at Bass River (1900), Hyannisport (1906), Marion (1906), Plymouth (1908), the Chatham Bars Inn (1914), Pocasset (1916), Wianno (1916), and Harwichport (1918). That doubled the number of courses already completed, and still more were in the planning.

Interest in the game of golf around Cape Cod, Nantucket & Martha's Vineyard roared throughout most of the 1920s with the opening of Eastward Ho! (1922) in Chathamport, The Edgartown Golf Club (1923) on the Vineyard, Sankaty Head Links (1923) on Nantucket, The Kittansett Club (1923) in Marion, Oyster Harbors (1927) in Osterville, both the Cape Cod Country Club (1929) and Cotuit Highground (1929) in Falmouth, and Chequessett Yacht & Country Club (1929) in Wellfleet. As the end of that legendary decade approached, the number of courses throughout the area had grown threefold since the very first days of just the Highlands Links, Seapuit, and Cummaquid.

Once limited to a fortunate few, the game was growing in popularity at a bewildering speed, and it was on the verge of becoming a business unto itself. In fact, conservative estimates were that nearly three million dollars had been spent on setting out courses. While that was certainly not a meager sum for the era, it was also an astounding amount to spend on developing a landscape which was so *naturally* suited to the game. Still, the returns proved to be great as golfers swarmed to this area, where folks might rightfully boast that there were more golf courses to the square mile than in any other region of America.

"Here, then," wrote one golfing enthusiast in 1928, "is a peninsula easily accessible, penetrated to the tip by railroad and highways, which offers the visitor almost everything he can ask for except mountains. It has the charm and atmosphere of an old land settled by the Pilgrim Fathers. It has expensive hotels and estates and simple boarding houses and little gray cottages converted into summer homes. It has the ocean bathing and still-water bathing, bay and deep-sea sailing, freshwater and deep-sea fishing. It has miles of fine roads and dim old byways through the inland forests. It has the gayest of summer resort life, and yet it is possible to tramp the outer beach or the interior woods for days and scarcely meet a soul. It has splendid sand-dunes and striking sea-cliffs, and it has intimate little tidewater inlets and marshes.

"It is impossible to imagine anywhere with more diversified scenes and pleasures," he concluded. "It is all things to all men, and the golfer is not the least of these."

Then came the Crash of '29.

The numbers of people having both the time and the money to devote to the game decreased with an indiscriminate vengeance.

The lesson fast learned was that organized golf clubs were vulnerable in the American economy. So great, in fact, was the impact upon golf throughout Cape Cod, Nantucket & Martha's Vineyard that only one course would be built in these parts between the time of the Great Depression and the Kennedy Administration. That was Mink Meadows (1936) on Martha's Vineyard. While only one new club was constructed, some fell victim to real estate values. Such was the fate of the layout called Seapuit in the Barnstable village of Osterville, as well as the one known as Tupancy on Nantucket. Seapuit had been a 9-hole layout designed by a Scotsman named Crawford, who was brought to the States for that specific project before the turn of the century. Eventually, a club was formed, and Seapuit Golf Club long enjoyed a good-natured rivalry with Cummaquid over the possession of an ornate challenge cup. The land that was Seapuit, however, eventually was divided into house lots. Tupancy, which was built in the 1920s, was also plowed under by developers on the island.

Just up the coast from Osterville, was Santuit in the Barnstable village of Cotuit. Santuit was a neat 9-holer not far from where The Willowbend Club (1988) stands today; however, an upscale condominium development occupies the very space where once Santuit's fairways spread.

Further along in Falmouth, were three other courses that almost as quickly came and went. The Menauhant Hotel was set on the neck of land just east of Washburn Island, and the Menauhant course itself lasted one or two summers around 1915. In one other village of Falmouth, was built Sippewissett Golf Club (1920), and the architectural team of Wayne Stiles and John van Kleek had begun construction of Falmouth Country Club (not the present day Falmouth Country Club) in 1928. That plan disappeared, however, not long after the stock market crash.

Further up the Cape once stood a golf club during the early part of this century with the especially colorful name of Ben Lomond (1912). Named for the fictional site of many short stories by P.G. Wodehouse, the 9-hole Sagamore course overlooked Cape Cod Canal and Cape Cod Bay. Meanwhile, across the bay to the east, a Bostonian with the equally colorful name of Quincy Shaw Adams built Cedar Bank (1923) alongside the Atlantic on his lower Cape estate. His 18-hole course stretched around Salt Pond, not far from where the National Seashore's Visitors Center now stands, and there Adams invited friends and golfing celebrities alike to play. These acquaintances included both Bobby Jones and his good friend, Francis Ouimet, winner of the 1913 US Open, who often came together. While Jones attended Harvard Law School in the 1920s, they not only visited Cedar Bank, but also played at Eastward Ho! and Highland Links. During the days, the friends played golf; at night, they played bridge in the rustic, Cedar Bank clubhouse.

As with all too many other local courses, though, the appealing value of house lots eventually reduced the original 18-hole course at Cedar Bank to 9 holes. As Adams aged and no longer could play his favorite game, Cedar Bank faded from existence by 1945. Most of the property today remains part of the Cape Cod National Seashore.

Meanwhile, even the strongest clubs remained susceptible through the Great Depression and beyond. Though Cummaquid Golf Club had enjoyed venerable beginnings, it nearly went out of existence after World War II until a group of members brought the club back to life.

Perhaps the Crash of '29 and its aftermath should have provided a stronger warning of the game's vulnerable existence when golf first bordered upon becoming a bustling business. As the esteemed English golf architect Herbert Fowler had once proclaimed: "God builds golf links, and the less man meddle, the better for all concerned." Having designed the legendary Westward Ho! course in the United Kingdom, Herbert Fowler later designed Eastward Ho! in Chathamport. From the very outset, Nature had done for golf on Cape Cod, Nantucket & Martha's Vineyard what elsewhere had required the investments of great fortunes to create.

To further appreciate and understand the game's original growth, as well as its resiliency on the Cape & Islands after the Crash of '29, you need only look to the very, very beginnings of this layout set down by the Master Designer. As Donald Ross had noted in a different context: "The Lord made golf courses. Golf architects simply discover them."

The Basic Layout

Before any hackers and duffers ever set foot upon this land, long before the Pilgrims and the Vikings came exploring, and even before the Wampanoags had gently trod their meandering footpaths along these virgin shores, the northern hemisphere had been a frozen lump.

Some ten thousand years ago, a great glacier pushed its way from the polar cap down through the lower latitudes, where the formidable force of this frozen water churned up topsoil, broke down boulders, and ground smaller rocks into gravel as it jumbled them together with mammoth blocks of ice. Ever so gently, it plowed a devastating southward course, and when its progress finally came to a halt, this immense sheet of ice had shouldered the surface of this particular corner of the world into a long, curling pile of earth and ice.

Then just as slowly, decades of warming caused the glacier to melt and retreat from these furthest advances, leaving in its wake mounds of soil and rocks, as well as massive chunks of ice. Wherever the water from those melting pieces of abandoned glacier held fast, seemingly bottomless ponds were created, but wherever the water evaporated, rolling depressions just as deep were left in the sandy landscape. These ponds and depressions became known as *kettles*, while the mounds became known as *moraines*. And all around these distinctive outcrops of land, the waters of the oceans gradually rose and filled the lowest outwash plains among all this glacial rubble.

That was how Nature created not only the peninsula we know as Cape Cod, but also the surrounding islands we call Nantucket, Martha's Vineyard, and the Elizabeths. From the highest moraines in Sandwich, Dennis, North Truro, and Sankaty Head to the outwash plains of Edgartown, this topography remains for the most part a sandy, hilly landscape, thickly forested with low-lying scrub oaks and pines. Ideal for the creation of golf courses, this particular piece of geography is unlike any other part of New England. Just over the top of a rolling hill, for example, a golfer will often come upon a gorgeous ocean view instead of the usual varied sweeps of pastoral green. Without a doubt, some of the loveliest views on all of the Cape & Islands are to be found just around the corners of a local golf course.

In addition to this characteristic topography, the weather and the climate across Cape Cod, Nantucket & Martha's Vineyard contribute their own competitive elements to every local round. The prevailing seaside winds certainly play a significant role in the growth of any golfer's game, and most pros will agree that they have developed an impressive repertoire of strokes just for coping with whatever winds might blow from the sounds, the bays, and the ocean. In fact, these wind conditions vary so greatly that even those club members whose play is practically all on one course encounter differing winds that add renewed interest to their game. These same winds have left their marks upon the landscape by keeping low the surrounding trees and vegetation. This is especially true on the moraines of North Truro and on Nantucket, whose heathered moors are most like the links of Scotland, where golf put down its earliest roots.

In addition to generating those distinctive winds, the nearby waters also tend to create moderate, comforting temperatures. Summers on Cape Cod, Nantucket & Martha's Vineyard tend to be more kind, while winters are generally less severe than in other parts of New England. The infrequent snows usually melt fast, and the sandy soil helps dry the fairways and the greens quite quickly. As a result, golf around these parts often lasts a month longer than it does in most parts of New England, and that helps swell the Cape & Islands' resident population of 200,000 to something more than a steady half million visitors on any given day in the summer. A staggering twelve million vacationers cross the Sagamore and Bourne bridges every year. Most of them have their golf bags in tow, because they are attracted to what still remains the largest concentration of golf courses in the United States north of the Mason-Dixon line.

Around Cape Cod, Nantucket & Martha's Vineyard, there are fifty courses: nearly eight hundred holes, the majority of which are open to the public. These courses range from chip-and-putt tracks to championship layouts, and they have played host to events that include the prestigious Walker Cup and the Ladies Professional Golf Association tour. There are public courses built by local towns, world-renown summer resort tracks, and entire residential community courses, as well as exclusive courses surrounded by vacation homes of the wealthy.

This growth of golf on Cape Cod, Nantucket & Martha's Vineyard has paralleled the expansion of golf on the mainland. In 1916, there were 742 courses in the United States; by 1923, there were 1,903; and by the Crash of '29, their number had grown to 5,648 golf clubs. After World War II, though, the number of courses had dwindled to a low of 4,817, and it was unable to surpass the 6,000-mark until 1960. Then, over the next two decades, that number had doubled to more than 12,000.

Since then, the number of courses in America increased again by more than 1,800. That averages out to three new courses opening every week. On the Cape & Islands, twelve courses have opened since 1980. Others, meanwhile, died on the drawing board, either for lack of financing during the economic slowdown, or else for a growing concern to preserve what little natural wildlife areas still remained on Cape Cod, Nantucket & Martha's Vineyard.

Despite this area's early interest in the game, as well as its rapid growth, not one club from the Cape & Islands was among the forty represented when the Massachusetts Golf Association (MGA) formed in February of 1903. The first club to associate with the MGA was The Hyannisport Club in 1907.

Many of the early golfers in these parts belonged to clubs in the

Boston area and the courses on Cape Cod, Nantucket & Martha's Vineyard were only their summer affiliations; however, these courses were fast becoming more than just simple summer clubs. Designed by true architects of golf who could not only establish legitimate distances, but also place challenging hazards that complied with tests of precision, more than a few of these courses would be championship layouts that penalized any golfer who played with poor form or without care. Of course (no pun intended), the game had not begun that way on the Cape.

Like a lot of the local lore, the truth behind the creation of Highland Links basically remains uncertain. The links might have been just another recreational diversion. Or it could have been created for the very same reason that courses would be built nearly a century later: to attract tourists with money to spend.

Since the middle of the 19th century, Isaac Morton Small and his family had operated the Highland House Hotel atop the windswept glacial moraine that is the high land called North Truro. The hotel was a summer resort not only for wealthy Bostonians, but also for elite families from throughout the Northeast. In the later part of that century, the expansion of the railroad lines had been creeping along Cape Cod toward Provincetown, and Small realized that these trains would bring more tourists to the lower Cape. So, he hoped to add some attraction other than the usual beaches and the boating.

When Small's son, Willard, returned from Yale College in 1892, he brought with him this new game that was all the rage: golf. Though the younger Small is known to have designed this original course, no one today can be sure which way the holes went, and nobody is certain whether only three holes opened one year, or when any other holes might have followed. For certain, though, golf did exist at Highland Links in 1892, and the course was open to the public. Some have claimed that this was the first public course in all of America; however, that's just not so. Those honors belong to Van Cortland in New York City and Franklin Park in Boston.

Like horseshoes or croquet, though, golf at Highland Links was just a game. There were no scorecards, and this game had no wooden tees. In fact, for the first twenty years the teeing areas were little more than sand and dirt. Before addressing the ball, a golfer would simply grab a handful of sand, make a small mound, then carefully place the ball upon it. Holes were no more than tin tomato cans buried in the ground, and most of the greens were hard-packed sand. In fact, one green was even made of cement. A frequent guest at the Highland House Hotel was a New York opera singer named J. Henry McKinley. An avid golfer, he was responsible for changing the greens from sand to sod in 1916. As golfers played around the cornfields and vegetable gardens, changes were made each year to the course. To this day, not much has changed at Highland Golf Links, and it remains a portal to another era when men in long coats played with clubs that had wooden shafts.

While Highland Links has ever remained in its time warp, a true links in the fashion of Royal St. George in Sandwich, England, various architects have continued to work their skills on this glacial landscape around Cape Cod, Nantucket & Martha's Vineyard. Donald Ross placed his imprint upon a handful of these courses, including: Oyster Harbors, Plymouth Country Club, Pocasset Golf Club, The Wianno Club, and Nantucket Golf Links.

There have even been stories that he built Cape Cod Country Club, as well as The Hyannisport Club, but those seem to be only stories. The Donald Ross Society has done extensive research work into courses that claim to be Donald Ross designs. Of the six hundred courses studied, the society has been able to prove or deny his involvement in all but six of them. One of those unresolved six is Cape Cod Country Club in Falmouth.

The Hyannisport Club, on the other hand, presents an interesting and verifiable tale involving a Donald Ross design. For years, golfers had regarded this course as a Ross masterpiece; however, that has been proven to be something less than fully true. While the club, indeed, engaged Ross to design a course along Nantucket Sound, Hyannisport balked when it reviewed his plans and saw the construction costs. The deal was dead.

Instead, the true architect of The Hyannisport Club is Frederick Paine, one of its original members. While utilizing some of the routing suggested by Ross, Paine and his workers did their best without having the consummate skills to build the fairways and the greens to the subtle specifications envisioned by Ross. So, the master architect's original drawings were stored away in the club's attic, where they remained until 1980, when greens superintendent Bob St. Thomas discovered them by chance.

In those early days of golf course architecture, there were several other distinguished architects who designed layouts for Cape Cod, Nantucket & Martha's Vineyard. Their names belong in a veritable *Who's Who* among such professionals:

• George C. Thomas, who had helped design both the Merion Cricket Club in Pennsylvania and the Pine Valley Golf Club in New Jersey, made his first solo attempt at golf course architecture just after the turn of the century when he designed Little Marion Golf Club;

• Herbert Fowler, considered the most creative designer in the days before Donald Ross, came to America in the 1920s and built Eastward Ho! Country Club in Chathamport;

• Devereaux Emmet, a founder of the National Golf Links on Long Island, worked along with his partner, Al Tull, to lay out Coonamesset in 1929. (During its existence this course was also called the Treadway and then Clausen's before it took on its current name of Cape Cod Country Club.);

• A.W. Tillinghast, builder of some of the world's great courses (Winged Foot Golf Club in New York and Baltusrol Golf Club in New Jersey), did some work on Nantucket's Sankaty Head Golf and Beach Club;

• Thomas Winton, a Scot who worked with architect Willie Park before going out on his own, designed Woods Hole Golf Club.

Among the collected works of all these distinctive architects, however, one course in particular stands out as an especially fine example of golf architecture: The Kittansett Club in Marion. Built alongside the sailing grounds of Buzzards Bay, Kittansett has remained the one and only work of Frederick C. Hood, and there are several reasons why his sole attempt has remained a great course in the eyes of some of the game's most reputable authorities, including *Golf Digest* and *Golf Magazine*.

In evaluating any layout, they take into consideration certain basics. One is *shot value*, the various risks and rewards involved in making good shots. Another is *resistance to scoring*, the degree of difficulty a course possesses while still remaining fair. *Design balance* includes the variety of hole layout, and *memorability* refers to how much of the course you can remember after you play it. After all, if the holes tend to blur together, then they obviously do not combine to create a memorable course. *Esthetics* involves the scenic value of the course, including not only how picturesque the shots might be in leading onto the greens, but also the ambience of the area. Finally, the element of *conditioning* takes into account the manicure of the fairways, the speed of the greens, and the overall condition of the course.

In applying these criteria to the one and only course that Hood had ever designed, the experts continue to rate Kittansett very high. For example, approach shots to the greens at Kittansett are a special nicety. If you hit a drive into the prescribed landing area, all your approach shots enable you to see the base of the flagstick. In addition, Kittansett's greens are always fast and true.

Though this has always been so since the course first opened in 1922, Kittansett remained isolated from the outside world until 1953, when it hosted the Walker Cup matches between the United States and Great Britain/Ireland. After that, international golf writers spread the word of Kittansett's virtues. The Massachusetts State Amateur also has been there three times, and the course's strengths have never diminished. To this day, *Golf Digest* considers Kittansett one of the Top 100 courses in America, while *Golf Magazine* lists the course among its own Top 100.

A Vanishing Breed

Just because the number of courses around Cape Cod, Nantucket & Martha's Vineyard had failed to grow much beyond Mink Meadows in those years between the Crash of '29 and the Kennedy Administration, that does not mean that interest in golf had flagged to any great extent. On the contrary, those involved with the game during that period can never forget the quiet beauty and historic charm that belonged to golf as much as it belonged to the Cape & Islands. And such recollections of that era are cherished no less by a special group of youngsters who each answered to the name of "caddie."

Back in Scotland, the term originally had been applied either to boys who ran errands, or else to men who undertook odd jobs. A form of the word *cadet*, *caddie* eventually came to be used more often than not for those who carried a golfer's clubs around the links, and that is how the word is used exclusively on this side of the North Atlantic.

From the 1920s into the 1960s practically every private course on the Cape & Islands seemed to have a caddie camp, be it a tent village or a Quonset hut. From Boston, from New York City, and from countless other urban areas throughout the northeast, hundreds of boys found their way by bus to summer quarters at the coastline courses, such as Sankaty Head, Oyster Harbors, Hyannisport,

Wianno, Coonamesset, and Eastward Ho! After staying for ten weeks, they would return home having not only a few more dollars in their pockets, but also a little more knowledge of life than when they had first arrived at camp.

Prior to World War II, the standard wage for a caddie camper was $2.50 to carry two bags around 18 holes. If he hustled, he might pick-up a quarter tip. This work was shared among the sixty or so boys, ranging in ages from nine to sixteen, who spent the summer at a caddie camp. Virtually every one of these camps had a caste system, however, and the pecking order was rigid: camp officer, squad leader, senior, intermediate, junior and blimp. The camp officers and squad leaders were much like camp counselors; the blimps were at the bottom of the pack.

Blimps were youngsters too young to caddie. More often than not, they were the younger brothers of caddie campers, and this was no more than a chance for them to get away from the city for the summer with their older brothers. The duties of a blimp were simple: keep the camp grounds clean and stay out of trouble.

"It wasn't easy getting into caddie camp," recalls Marshfield's Joe Coughlin of his days at Osterville's Wianno Club back in the 1930s. "It was easier getting into Harvard."

Coughlin had a couple of things going for him. First, no caddie could get into any camp unless he had a blood relative who had caddied at the camp, and Coughlin's uncle had been at Wianno. Second, his family lived in the same Boston area neighborhood as Ray Faxon, who ran several caddie camps, including Coonamesset, Woods Hole, and Oyster Harbors. Years later, Faxon would be also become known as the grandfather of PGA Tour player Brad Faxon, one of many professional players to learn the game on Cape Cod.

When Coughlin began his caddying at Wianno in 1931, he was eleven. As a junior in the caste system, he was entitled to earn sixty cents for 9 holes; for 18 holes, a dollar. There was no tipping at Wianno, and there were no tees. "There was a box of sand," recalls Coughlin, and you'd grab a handful and neatly pile it on the ground. Then, you placed your player's ball on top of it." This was part of that beauty and charm.

Now gone forever, the caddie camp at Wianno that charged each caddie a dollar a day for room and board was just to the right of the 17th fairway. Kids like Coughlin had to make money, and young Joe might have been able bring home $50 for a summer of caddying. For any kid who grew-up in the Depression years, that was good money: enough to buy back-to-school clothes.

In turn, a caddie's daily rent bought mixed benefits. At Wianno, for example, every morning at six all the caddies took a swim in the lake. "They gave you a bar of soap," explains Coughlin, "and you'd go into the water bare-ass and wash." And though it sometimes was cold that early in a summer's morning, the dip was the prelude to a substantial breakfast, where caddies always ate well for the dollar it had cost them. Always there was cereal and eggs, plus all the toast and jam a kid could want. And there was plenty of milk.

At Faxon's Coonamesset caddie camp, there was even a special meal at the end of each season when Polcari's Restaurant of Boston catered a spread for the boys, most of whom came from the neighboring North Bennett Street Industrial School.

Altogether, these camps had good men operating them. They gave each caddie one day off in the week, and they did their best to make certain that everyone had an opportunity to caddie. Wianno, for instance, maintained a revolving list so that no boy was ever among the first caddies out two days in a row. Wherever the list of assignments might have stopped on one day would be the spot where the caddie master would begin on the following morning.

After supper, the caddies were allowed to play five holes on the back 9, far away from the clubhouse, and often they would play against other caddies from Woods Hole, Hyannisport, and Oyster Harbors. In addition, camps often held competitions among one another in events like swimming, diving, and baseball, all of which have been woven into a mosaic of memories, some even greater than others.

"I remember right after the 1932 Olympics, Babe Didriksen, came to Wianno," says Coughlin. "She played with our pro, Ray Bronson, and I'm glad I didn't have to carry her bag. After she hit a shot, she'd dash to her ball," he says. "I don't mean hurry. I mean *run*. She had a big bag, and I thought her caddie was going to have a heart attack just trying to keep up with her."

And then there was the annual visit by Massachusetts Governor

James Michael Curley to Wianno, which was a restricted club with a wealthy, conservative membership. "You know," explains Coughlin, "No Irish Need Apply. No Jewish members, either. But what were they going to do?" he asks. "Say 'no' to the Governor of the Massachusetts? He'd probably have found a way to close them down."

The caddies looked forward to Curley's Labor Day visit, complete with an entourage of twelve or sixteen golfers. Though most would have admitted that the Governor was "just a hacker" when it came to the game, Curley loved golf nonetheless. The games really began, though, when the last of Curley's foursomes finished on the 18th green. That's when the Governor would take out a $5 bill, and place it on the green. Then all the caddies would putt for the Governor's prize.

When Coughlin left Wianno after three years to take a summer job in Boston for $10 a week, he took with him a wealth of priceless memories. Having been at caddie camp, he understands that it was a special part of life that he can never, ever experience again. And thanks to the advent of the mechanical golf cart neither can many other youngsters.

Those golf carts began appearing at clubs on the Cape & Islands in the late 1950s. In the '60s, they encroached on caddies, and by the 1970s carts were more popular. Shortly thereafter, the caddie camps faded away on the Cape.

For caddies who came in the twilight of those years, though, the 1960s made the experience no less exciting when the Kennedys walked the fairways of Hyannisport. Such was the case with James Riley, who went on to become a Boston insurance executive. Like Coughlin some thirty years earlier, Riley considered his years at caddie camp in the 1960s to have been the best thing that ever could have happened to a youngster.

Most of the caddies at Hyannisport were hockey players, because the camp director was Bill Hutchinson, a guidance counselor and hockey coach at Quincy High School. Riley had played hockey at Boston Technical High School, came to know Hutchinson, and that is how he found his way into the camp.

Hyannisport's caddies slept eight to a tent in the camp set down between the 11th and 12th holes, and every morning the pro shop would call down and tell them just how many caddies were needed. While twenty or so would usually go out to carry bags, everyone else would clean the camp for inspection.

By the 1960s, a caddie was paid $4 for carrying singles and $8 for doubles, and Hyannisport charged its caddies $20 a week for room and board. Meanwhile, each caddie at camp had a notebook to keep a diary of whom he had caddied for and when. That was every boy's way of understanding just how much he was financially ahead or behind.

"On Friday night they would get us all together, and they would announce how much everyone made," Riley explains. "If you didn't earn enough to pay for your room and board, you were *In the Hole*," he says. "Nobody wanted to be *In the Hole*."

In addition to the work, though, there was also some organized fun. Before dusk every evening, the caddies could play as much golf as they wanted; however, they couldn't cross the bridge that separated the inside five holes from the rest of the course. And one night a week was "Scrounge Night," when the caddies combined work and play by putting on their bathing suits and digging through the muddy swamps along the water holes for lost balls. The pro would sell the good ones as second-hand balls, and the rest went out to the driving range.

From his three-year stint as a caddie at Hyannisport, James Riley still possesses a trophy of sorts: a pair of Foot-Joy golf shoes given to him by Peter Lawford, the film star who was married to Patricia Kennedy.

The Kennedys often played late in the afternoons, and whenever the call came to the pro shop, the caddies were told to put on their our cleanest pants and best shirts, then go up to the 1st tee.

The Kennedys rarely played in foursomes. Instead, they generally played in bunches of sixsomes, but there was never anybody else out on the course so it really did not matter.

"One day, Peter Lawford didn't have any golf shoes, so he bought a new pair of Foot-Joys," Riley tells his story. "After they finished playing, Lawford changed into his regular shoes and forgot the new ones when he left the pro shop. The pro told me to pick them up and catch him in the parking lot."

So, Riley raced outside to the parking lot and yelled to Lawford.

"What size do you wear?" Lawford turned and asked Riley.

"A nine," replied the caddie. "Nine-and-a-half."

"Then keep them," Lawford answered as he got into the Lincoln Continental to drive away. "They're yours now."

And so they have been ever since.

Yet another distinguished alumnus of the Hyannisport caddie camp is Jamaica Plain's Paul Stewart, now a National Hockey League referee, who has carried with him forever a different sort of reminder. One time a golfer threw a club at the young Stewart, and the caddie promptly took the guy's bag right over to a nearby creek and heaved it into the water. Though, the guy was a guest, Stewart could not have cared any less, for if caddying did nothing else, it certainly taught Stewart a lesson about the disposition of people.

In contrast, of sorts, to Stewart's encounter, however, was that of Dorothy Small Garfield, a grand niece of I.M. Small, who had owned The Highland Golf Links. When Garfield was a young girl during the 1930s, her job was to collect greens fees. And though she could still clearly recall those summer days when the immortal Bobby Jones would come to play at Highland Links, what she most fondly recounts is the time that the entire Eastern Fleet dropped anchor in Provincetown Harbor for a week.

"A lot of the Naval officers came over to play golf," she tells, "and there was one young officer left over, so I went out to play a round with him."

As golfers, the sailors were slow, and Dorothy kept getting impatient to hit. Finally, on one hole, she thought they were out of the way, and she uncorked an especially impressive drive. The problem, though, was that it hit one of the officers in the foursome just ahead.

"Oh, you should have heard the fellow I was with," she says. "He kept yelling, *You hit the Admiral! You hit the Admiral!*"

The Admiral, on the other hand, kept his composure when he saw that the errant golfer was a sixteen-year-old girl.

Now, two or three generations after that, the last surviving caddie camp on the Cape & Islands remains at Sankaty Head on Nantucket, where some forty or so campers still spend ten weeks of their summer in a precarious coexistence among a fleet of golf carts. These caddies pay $5 per night for room and board in a Quonset hut, and in addition to toting clubs for a round of 18 holes, they still perform other tasks: always there are bathrooms to clean and bushes to manicure, neither of which a golf cart has yet demonstrated any ability to do. With some hard work, a caddie can go home with a couple of thousand dollars, as well as an opportunity to earn a share of more than $25,000 in college scholarships offered to prized youngsters.

And, of course, a priceless collection of memories.

One Brief Shining Moment

Things changed dramatically for local golf in the 1960s. The construction of courses resumed with renewed vigor throughout Cape Cod, Nantucket & Martha's Vineyard. The Kennedy family gained prominence. And camps for caddies, as the Cape & Islands had come to know them, were about to face a certain extinction.

The caddie program finally began to fade out of the picture at Hyannisport about the time that Tom Niblet had become the head professional. In fact, during his first year at the 'Port in 1961, the club brought in its first six golf carts. Each year thereafter more carts were added to that number until caddies finally disappeared altogether in 1970. "You hate to see changes like that," Niblet admits, "and it happened very quickly."

He had taken over as the golf professional at Hyannisport during the same month that the people of the United States had elected John F. Kennedy as President. Back then, not everyone understood that the Kennedys originally had moved to Hyannisport more or less because of golf. Prior to that, Joseph P. Kennedy had taken his family on their summer retreat to Hull, just south of Boston. When the elder Kennedy had tried to join the Cohasset Golf Club in 1923, however, he was blackballed by the purely Yankee club membership that practiced a widely-applied Brahmin principle succinctly known as *NINA*: No Irish Need Apply. So commonplace was that term in those days that *NINA* readily appeared in classified advertisements throughout the Boston newspapers.

Understanding full well, then, that he simply was not welcome, Joe Kennedy took his family to Cape Cod. Though Hyannisport was yet another Yankee stronghold, Joe Kennedy had helped many of its members through tough economic times, and here he was able to secure admission. As a result, the Kennedy family grew up on the golf course, where they still kept generally to themselves. None of the Kennedy family was ever especially loved at this staunch conservative Republican haunt, and the club even discharged head professional Walter Hall in 1960, because his friendship with the Kennedys irritated the old members at Hyannisport.

And while all of the Kennedys had a genuine interest in the game of golf, Tom Niblet did not see much of the new President during his first year as the pro at Hyannisport. Jack Kennedy had aggravated his back injury at a tree-planting ceremony in Toronto, so he did not play much golf in 1961. Instead, he would walk up just to watch Jacqueline taking lessons, or else to be with the others from the family who were playing on the inside 9.

"If the members at Hyannisport knew about my affection for the man, I probably would have lost my job," says Niblet. "It was exciting just being around the man," he adds. "John Kennedy was charismatic. Everything about him just energized you. He'd look you in the eye and show interest in what you said."

Somewhat ironically, in fact, Jack Kennedy had kept his golf game almost a secret for a long time, because the sport at that time had been more readily associated with Republicans, an image often underscored by Ike's personal passion for the game. Nonetheless, Jack Kennedy had always possessed the right coordination, but his bad back had made it painful to perform even the simplest of the game's fundamentals: placing the ball on the tee and taking it out of the cup.

Tom Niblet still tells the stories of those late Friday afternoons when he would watch a military helicopter from Otis Air Force Base land at the Kennedy Compound, then he would wait for the phone to ring.

"First, he would ask if it was busy up there?" says Niblet. "I'd say, *No, it isn't, Mr. President.*"

Then the President of the United States would come up the hill with his golf shoes, pants and shirt in hand; however, he never came into the clubhouse. JFK would change his clothes in the bag room, where he kept his clubs and a special White House telephone. In there, Niblet says, the Secret Service would take the President's clubs out of the bag and turn it upside down, just for safety precautions. Then, the Secret Service would get their own golf bags. Instead of golf clubs, though, those bags held machine guns, just in case.

In early spring of 1961, Niblet received yet another interesting call from someone wanting to speak with the golf pro.

"Yes," he replied, "I'm Mr. Niblet."

To which, the caller continued: "I'm Mrs. John Kennedy, and I'd like to take some golf lessons."

At that point, Niblet did not know what to say. It might have been a prank, so at first he did not say a thing. Then again, he thought, it could have been Mrs. Kennedy, but he was not sure. So, he bought some time with a fib: he told her there were no openings that morning, and he made an appointment for an afternoon golf lesson.

As three o'clock rolled around, the Lincoln Continental appeared, and Mrs. Kennedy walked into the pro shop. Tom Niblet introduced himself, and she told him that he might be in for a difficult time trying to teach her to play golf.

"I didn't think so," he said.

The President's wife explained that she had taken a few lessons in Newport, but had never really become involved in the game. Still, she said that she had really enjoyed it.

As the lessons came and passed, Mrs. Kennedy did prove to be well-coordinated, but Tom Niblet recalls that she never developed her talent. "She might play five holes or the inside 9," he still remembers. "Then she would say to me: *Tom, how come my game doesn't improve?*

"The answer is simple," the pro told her. "Quit water skiing and tennis and horseback riding. Devote some time to the game of golf and you'll improve.

"She wasn't going to give them up," he admits, "but she did continue to enjoy golf."

That was all part of those summers in Camelot, when the caddies and the Kennedys still strolled the fairways, when somebody famous was always coming and going, and when the press and the public alike were always trying to catch a glimpse of the President and the First Lady.

One afternoon, Jack Kennedy came off the 18th green quite disgusted. He told Tom Niblet that he had played terribly, and he asked if Tom might have some time the next day for a lesson. They scheduled a lesson for nine the next morning.

When the time arrived, though, Kennedy called Niblet and said something else had come up. He asked if he could have some time later, and the golf pro said he would keep the afternoon open for the President. Unbeknownst to Niblet and to most of the world, the United States was in the midst of an international incident in Laos.

"A few minutes later, I looked out on the golf course," Niblet says, "and I saw three huge Marine helicopters land on the edge of the 14th fairway."

From the helicopters toward the summer White House emerged a seemingly endless entourage of White House advisors, including Secretary of Defense Robert S. McNamara and General Robert Maxwell of the Joint Chiefs.

"He had all these problems," remarks Niblet with an air of wonderment toward the President, "and he made the time to call to say he couldn't make a golf lesson."

Then later that afternoon, Tom Niblet saw the black Lincoln Continental convertible coming across the causeway toward The Hyannisport Club. The President was driving, and with him was his close friend, Chuck Spalding, an investment banker from New York, who had a 4- or 5-handicap. Into the shop the two of them walked, and the President asked Niblet if he were busy. When the pro said he wasn't, Kennedy replied: "Well let's go knock it around a few holes."

Meanwhile, the President's press secretary, Pierre Salinger, had lost his own clubs on the flight from Washington and was using Niblet's bag somewhere out on the course. So, Niblet grabbed another set and went out for a round with the President.

"We went out to the 1st tee," says Niblet. "I teed it up and hit it over the hill. Spalding hit next and knocked it about five yards past my ball."

The President looked at Niblet, looked at Spalding, then he put his driver back in the bag and took out his 5-wood.

"You know," said Kennedy, "I never wanted to be a big driver. I just like to be with big hitters."

This all took place in 1963, just after the US Open had been held at The Country Club that previous June, and the threesome played Hyannisport's inside 9: the 1st, 2nd, 3rd, 4th and 5th of the front 9, as well as the 15th, 16th, 17th and 18th of the back 9. At one point, the President turned to Spalding and said: "The Country Club. I don't think there is a club with more cheapskates in America."

Not many months later, the President was dead.

"When he died," says Niblet, "so did a little bit of me."

Niblet had also known Bobby Kennedy as a golfer, a big hitter, long and strong. He always played with three or four members of his family, a kid on his shoulders, and maybe a couple of dogs.

"He was a family guy," remembers Niblet. "Seldom played without them. And if he wasn't playing with his family, it was with some special guests."

One time Niblet was giving a lesson to Nancy Salinger, the wife of JFK's press secretary, and they began walking across the bridge by the 3rd tee. Coming off the 2nd green was Bobby Kennedy, along with his wife, Ethel, and their guests. The pro was certain that he knew one player's face, but couldn't quite place him.

"Have you met John Glenn?" asked Kennedy.

At that point in Niblet's career at Hyannisport, the experience had become a frequent one.

In retrospect, those Kennedy years had signaled not only a waking-up of America, but also another vigorous phase of golf course construction on Cape Cod, Nantucket & Martha's Vineyard. In fact, when Tom Niblet eventually left Hyannisport, he did so to construct a course of his own not so very far away.

Good Day at Blue Rock

Over the course of the next generation, golf on Cape Cod, Nantucket & Martha's Vineyard evolved from being a recreational pastime of the rich and famous into a business that responded to the wishes of a wide spectrum of customers looking for their own special kind of leisure. Before the Cape & Islands was able to celebrate the first century of the game upon its fairways, golf had brought together the old and the young, the locals and the visitors, the wealthy and the commonfolk alike, and it even gave the local townships reason to rally behind them. After all, golf not only gave towns added reason to protect vast tracts of land from being subdivided into house lots, but also it held the promise of generating millions of dollars in newfound revenues. Still, the wheels of progress needed a starting nudge.

The first course built after the Great Depression was in 1962 at Blue Rock in South Yarmouth, the beginning of a new era. To fully understand the unqualified success of this course from the very outset, though, you must keep in mind the state of golf on the Cape & Islands in the late 1950s, a time when there still were very few golf carts.

Architect Geoffrey Cornish realized that senior citizens wanted to play golf, but that regulation courses often proved too strenuous. In addition, the existing courses were also too difficult for beginning players. What Cornish achieved with Blue Rock was to make golf available for those who could not cope physically with the longer, more difficult courses.

Employing the basics of strategic design and maintenance that had long been applied to the bigger courses, he proved that a diminished course could still call for every club in the bag and could demand fine turfgrass as well. Thus was created Blue Rock, a diminished championship course of 2,770 yards that offered 18 holes, ranging from 103 yards to 247. And it would occupy only 45 acres.

Some historians want to label Blue Rock as one of the first par-3 courses ever in existence; however, there had already been plenty of others dating back into the 1920s. In fact, Cornish had grown up on one in western Canada. As with countless others, many of these abbreviated courses disappeared because of the Great Depression and then the war.

Shorter than regulation courses, the so-called *executive courses* may have a few par-4s or even a par-5, but basically they consist of par-3 holes. Once they began being built during the 1960s on the Cape, they proved extremely popular among both of Cornish's targeted groups of golfers: beginners and senior citizens. While these people might otherwise have suffered an arduous journey trying to make a par or birdie on a traditional layout's 550-yard par-5 with two carries over water hazards, they would find an executive course not nearly as difficult. Instead, executive courses became wonderful places for novices to learn the game, as well as for senior citizens to carry on their skills with a respectable, yet relaxed challenge. Here an occasional par and even a birdie remained within grasp.

The year after Blue Rock opened, another executive course opened in Wareham, called Little Harbor, which became quite popular with the golfers who lived south of Boston. Often when their own courses were covered with snow at home, they discovered that Wareham (as well as the rest of the Cape & Islands) generally did not have snow. Places such as Little Harbor, then, were found to be open for play throughout the year.

While there were other courses sprouting up, such as the Otis Golf Course (1963) and Nantucket's Miacomet (1963), The

Falmouth Country Club (1964) and The Country Club of New Seabury (1964), as well as Dennis Pines (1965) and Bay Pointe (1965), by the time that 1966 rolled around Hyannisport's Tom Niblet realized the increasing popularity of par-3 courses, and he was eager to make a move.

Already Niblet had proven that he knew as much about building courses as he did about playing golf. During the 1950s, he and Alex Ohlson had built the Norton Country Club from scratch. So, he convinced Hyannisport's superintendent, Gene McCarthy, that they should both leave Hyannisport and build a course of their own. Niblet found a suitable piece of land on the Sandwich moraine, and they hired Geoffrey Cornish to design a course that would prove to be no less in stature than the one he had constructed at Blue Rock. That was the beginning of Holly Ridge.

At that same time, there were two other par-3 projects under way. One that opened was called Fiddler's Green, which is now the Tara Woods. The other was called Ashumuth Valley, now the Paul Harney Golf Club in Hatchville.

Even if Niblet had known those two other par-3s were being built and about to open, he believes that he still would have built Holly Ridge. "You go into these projects with blinders on," he says in retrospect. "You become too committed." Still, his timing could not have been any worse.

Besides having to compete for golfers, Holly Ridge opened during a period of high interest rates that continued to slow the entire economy. Then came the oil embargo, followed by the gas shortage that dissuaded golfers from driving to the Cape & Islands just to play a round of golf.

What kept Holly Ridge afloat during those lean times, however, was the concept that had placed this golf course alongside a senior citizen housing community. Though it might well have been easier to have abandoned the idea of a golf course and to have subdivided the land into house lots, the people behind the concept of Holly Ridge were committed.

Slowly times improved, and other courses continued to appear. Sam Volpe started Round Hill (1971) in Sandwich, the military restored Otis Golf Course (1973), Cranberry Valley (1974) opened in Harwich, Woodbriar (1974) appeared in Falmouth, and Iyanough

Hills (1974) began at what is now called Hyannis. During the year of the nation's Bicentennial, the Island Golf Links (1976) began as a 9-hole course on the Vineyard where Farm Neck now sits, and another 9-holer called Quashnet Valley opened in Mashpee.

Less than a decade later, Quashnet Valley already had expanded to 18 holes as the mega-boom hit in 1985. By then, you didn't have to be a research scientist to figure out the force behind it, either. All you had to do was try to get a tee time anywhere on Cape Cod, Nantucket or Martha's Vineyard.

One of the better public courses on the Cape & Islands came about simply because a Brewster hairdresser named Leona Leary had a customer miss an appointment, and that left her alone in her shop with time to think about what she had suffered the previous day.

Tired of waiting for a tee time at the old 9-hole Brewster Greens Golf Course the day before, Leary left the course and was fortunate to get one at Cranberry Valley in Harwich. And while she was playing, she was impressed by the beauty of it all.

Later, while cutting hair at Leona's Beauty Salon, she heard about plans for a proposed development of one hundred and fifty house lots on a certain parcel of land in Brewster.

"All I could think of was an extra hundred and fifty washing machines, another hundred and fifty toilets flushing, another hundred and fifty youngsters in our overpacked school," she says. "I thought it would be better to put a public golf course there instead of a hundred and fifty homes."

So, Leona Leary called the town selectmen, who told her she would need a hundred signatures to petition for a special town meeting about a golf course. The next day, she had one hundred and twenty-six without skipping a customer. Two days later, when she brought the petition to the selectmen, she had more than two hundred names.

As word spread around Brewster, the town gave the green light for a study committee to begin work on the project. Before much longer, Brewster passed a two million dollar bond issue, then hired Geoffrey Cornish and Brian Silva to design a regulation course on 167 acres just off Route 6.

The Brewster story symbolizes a significant golf boom on the

Cape & Islands. This boom, however, was not a simple, chain reaction. No, this boom more closely resembled nuclear fission, as other communities, including Dennis, Harwich, Chatham and Yarmouth, simultaneously were either planning, or else building new courses. They all were willing to finance public courses despite the lagging economy as well as the state-imposed restrictions upon property tax rates.

Clearly, the public's demand for golf had triggered this reaction. In the late 1970s, public courses on the Cape & Islands had been forced each day to turn away as many as two hundred prospective customers, many of whom had to take their clubs and recreation dollars back across the canal.

Nothing, however, makes a town open its coffers like the sight of an unhappy visitor departing Cape Cod, Nantucket or Martha's Vineyard. That is especially true if that visitor has money to spend but nowhere to spend it.

The Town of Dennis was far ahead of any other community in facing this situation on Cape Cod, and they built a second public course, Dennis Highlands, in 1985, the same year that Brewster had opened The Captains. The difference, however, was that the town's first public course, Dennis Pines (1965) was able to carry most of the debt service for the new course. Still, The Pines was feeling the squeeze with almost a thousand members who alternated starting times with visitors. Just as it was at Cranberry Valley, Dennis Pines had to turn people away. And so did Bass River in neighboring Yarmouth.

The existing town-owned course, Bass River already had some twelve hundred members and could not accommodate all the daily fee players who came in off-the-street. So, the Town of Yarmouth, which twice in the late 1970s had turned down a projected second course to complement Bass River, finally agreed to build another.

Besides, the town had the land, 180 acres. With the real estate market going crazy in the early 1980s, Bass River's pro Walter Hewins figured if Yarmouth didn't do it then, there would never be another chance to build that second course.

Further down the Cape in the Town of Chatham, home of the exclusive courses at Chatham Bars Inn (1914) and Eastward Ho! (1922), a committee had been studying the feasibility of a town-owned course when it decided in 1989 to purchase the Chatham Bars Inn layout and make it a public course named The Seaside Links of Chatham.

After less than a decade, Harwich began to consider a 9-hole addition to its popular course, Cranberry Valley, while the town of Barnstable opened Olde Barnstable Fairgrounds (1993) in Marstons Mills. During that same summer, the town of Falmouth was negotiating with Falmouth Country Club to purchase the facility and make it a town-owned course.

Despite the obvious enthusiasm that had generated all this action, however, not every plan for a golf course was able to come to fruition.

The New Beginning

While the number of public golf courses around Cape Cod, Nantucket & Martha's Vineyard was exploding at a pace that could match the era prior to the Crash of '29, there were even more plans on the drawing boards for private, upscale courses. The standard was established in the New Seabury area of Mashpee for the concept of surrounding golf courses not only with homes, but also with an entire community: retail stores, postal facilities, and even a governing body of sorts. Thereafter, almost everything else in residential concepts could have seemed somewhat anti-climactic.

Still, a review of things reveals that golf had come full circle and almost needed to reinvent itself in some ways. Whereas, in the beginning the game was played only by those with the time and money to be able to afford such recreation, almost a century of golf had made it a game of the people. Consequently, there had to be some new allure to re-create an exclusive upper tier, a tier that little to do with skill and everything to do with wealth. What then followed around provided an air of grandeur in its own right.

Just north of the Cape Cod Canal, for example, the Granger Building Systems of Worcester purchased the dormant White Cliffs Golf Course in the Cedarville section of Plymouth back in 1986. They bulldozed the course under altogether, then hired PGA Tour legend Gary Player to build an entirely new layout along the western shore of Cape Cod Bay. By the time the design was completed, the new White Cliffs Country Club could boast of a magnificent clubhouse, as well as a year-round residential community of single family homes, patio homes and townhouses set along the cliffs that rise some 200 feet above the water's edge.

Just opposite the western entrance of the Cape Cod Canal in Wareham, the Four Pines/Bay Pointe Corporation of Lexington purchased the old Wareham Golf Course from the town in 1987 for a million dollars. Headed by Louis Perez and Ulysses Bourque, Bay Pointe planned to make extensive changes in the golf course, envisioned a hotel with a convention center by the shores of Buzzards Bay, and wanted to build luxury townhouses. In addition, they hoped to establish a 100-room Victorian inn, as well as a two million dollar clubhouse with tennis courts and a swimming pool.

Meanwhile, much further down the Cape in Brewster, the Ocean Edge Resort already had sprung to life in 1986 on the site of the old 9-hole Brewster Greens Golf Course. Ocean Edge did everything it could to promote the resort. It not only hosted the New England PGA Championship for five years, but it also sponsored tennis tournaments, and even brought in Boston *Celtic* Kevin McHale to promote the golf course. From the outset, they planned what they wanted to do, then executed the plan very well.

In Mashpee, Bob St. Thomas, the greens superintendent at Hyannisport, dreamed of putting together his own upscale, residential community with its own private golf club facility called Willowbend. Though the course itself had its marks of distinction that included several heroic holes that play over water, as well as along cranberry bogs, the residential element of his concept for Willowbend soon would run into the same sorts of financial nightmares that plagued many in the late 1980s.

Willowbend's problems, though, were nothing like those which developed in North Falmouth. By 1989, Texan Steve Harrison had his own blueprint for another upscale development in there that called for two 18-hole golf courses, a mammoth 35,000 square-foot clubhouse, tennis courts, and more than two hundred sprawling homesites. He lured television commentator Dave Marr away from his job at Pebble Beach in California to be the director of golf, and he brought in architect Pete Dye to start his golf course.

Dye and Harrison walked the Falmouth Woods property and figured out a preliminary routing plan; however, Dye wanted his son, P.B. Dye, to be the architect of record, while Harrison did not. He wanted the elder Dye for his name value. Since they could not agree, they parted, and Harrison built the course himself.

About the same time not so far away in South Sandwich, Tom Niblet saw what had been happening throughout New England, and he was preparing for it. Members at off-Cape clubs, such as The Country Club in Brookline, Brae Burn in Newton and Pine Brook in Weston were aging and preparing to retire. Niblet knew that many of them wouldn't like Florida and would want to remain in New England, most likely on the Cape & Islands.

But Niblet also recognized that the clubs that these new retirees most likely would want to join, such as Oyster Harbors and Hyannisport, already were oversubscribed with long waiting lists. So, he hired nationally renowned architect Robert von Hagge to design a championship golf course called The Ridge Club, which Niblet describes as "an elegant and expensive place to call home."

Then the unthinkable happened.

The economy hit a buzzsaw, and recession ripped through the Cape & Islands, as well as the rest of New England. The town-owned courses proved to be in a position to more easily ride out the lagging economy of the 1990s; however, the newly-constructed private courses found themselves in a bind.

Some courses were never built. Rees Jones, who had done so much work at The Country Club in 1988 for the US Open, designed a 27-hole world class facility in Plymouth. Located just off Route 3, the site with more than 600 acres called Forges Field never got off the ground. In addition, both Chilton Hall and Head of the Bay in Plymouth, as well as an unnamed project in Mattapoisett never saw their first rounds of golf.

Other courses, such as White Cliffs and Ocean Edge, the first of the development courses, withstood best. The reason was simple. Both entered the market early, then stayed with intended plans.

But Steve Harrison's dream of Ballymeade disappeared into thin air when the substance of his plan was revealed as little more than the sort of smoke and mirrors that had typified a great many of the real estate and bank dealings of the late 1980s. After

Ballymeade filed for bankruptcy in March of 1990, it was taken over by the Bank of New England, which had loaned twenty-seven million dollars for the 900-acre spread. Eventually, though, the Bank of New England collapsed, too.

Shortly thereafter, Stephen and Patricia Harrison were charged with a hundred counts of bank fraud in connection with their loans from the Bank of New England. They were also charged with skimming more than a half million dollars in membership fees and using the money to buy a Lincoln Continental, to pay the sales tax on a Ferrari, and to rent a condominium at the Ritz-Carlton in Boston. About the only good aspect of the Harrisons' venture into the world of golf is that their involvement was atypical of anything else on Cape Cod, Nantucket & Martha's Vineyard.

Come the 1990s, a flurry of financial activities helped other golf dreams to remain in play.

In 1990, for example, a sixteen million dollar loan to The Willowbend Club was foreclosed upon by the Sentry Bank of Hyannis only days before federal regulators seized the bank itself. By April of 1991, however, Reebok chief executive Paul Fireman had purchased The Willowbend Club from the Resolution Trust Corporation, and his ownership all but guaranteed that Willowbend would become a first class operation. In time, much of the concept envisioned by St. Thomas began to fully bloom.

By the spring of 1993, a group of investors purchased the Ballymeade property for six million dollars, and things took a turn for the better. Almost immediately, they hired Chi Chi Rodriguez and Jim Fazio to make the course more playable.

Unfortunately, in Wareham BayBank had to foreclose on Bay Pointe after a new clubhouse was constructed, some condominiums were built, and only a few course renovations had been completed. Meanwhile, the convention center, the inn, and the hotel remained little more than a dream. Then, in the fall of 1993, BayBank agreed to sell the golf course for just over three million dollars to Onset Bay, Incorporated, headed by Bob and Rusty Gunnarson, two professionals from North Hill Country Club of Duxbury.

When all was said and done in the rocky transition from the 1980s into the 1990s, this generation of golf enthusiasts and architects indeed had discovered a whole new world of golf in the glacial landscape that is Cape Cod, Nantucket & Martha's Vineyard. Without a doubt, the most prolific of these architects has been Geoffrey Cornish, who can claim to have built more courses on the Cape & Islands than any other designer. Of the three hundred or so courses to his credit, Cornish has had his hand in the creation of eleven different courses on Cape Cod, Nantucket & Martha's Vineyard.

After his pioneering work on the par-3 Blue Rock in 1961, he went on to build the old White Cliffs course in Plymouth, the Tara in Hyannis, Holly Ridge Golf Club in South Sandwich, Woodbriar in Falmouth, Cranberry Valley in Harwich, Hyannis Golf Course, Quashnet Valley Country Club in Mashpee, and Farm Neck Golf Club in Oak Bluffs on the Vineyard. In addition, Cornish had collaborated with Brian Silva in the construction of Bayberry Hills in Yarmouth, The Captains in Brewster, Kings Way in Yarmouthport, Ocean Edge in Brewster, and the Olde Barnstable Fairgrounds in Marstons Mills.

As with the original boom of golf course construction before the Crash of '29, this generation of architects has its own roster of greats whose visions have enhanced the Cape & Islands. In addition to Cornish, these include:

• Dr. Michael Hurdzan, an Ohio architect, designed Dennis Highlands Golf Course and The Willowbend Club;

• Rees Jones, who reconstructed The Country Club before the 1988 US Open and who is the son of Robert Trent Jones, helped reconstruct The Country Club of New Seabury;

• Robert von Hagge, who played on the PGA Tour before creating more than 200 courses around the world, designed The Ridge Club (where he has a home site behind the 1st green);

• The Mitchell brothers, sons of legendary Robert Mitchell, all have worked on the Cape: Henry designed Dennis Pines and expanded Cummaquid; William created both courses at New Seabury; and Sam helped lay out Little Harbor in Wareham;

• Gary Player, one of the great PGA Tour players, designed the present White Cliffs Country Club course in Plymouth;

• Pete Dye, designer of Crooked Stick in Indiana and Long Cove at Hilton Head, did a preliminary routing of Ballymeade Country Club in North Falmouth.

The Once & Future Kingdom

Since its very beginnings more than a century ago, the game of golf on Cape Cod, Nantucket & Martha's Vineyard has become more than simply a source of recreation. Golf has become nothing less than a way of life. Make no mistake about it. This has manifested itself as an inner drive that draws Americans all across the greater northeast out in the dead of winter to search for snowless fairways.

Whenever the cold arrives in other parts of the region, the Cape & Islands become the last resort for the golf-hungry. Just ask any hardened golf addict who feels compelled to spend five or six hours trekking by car from either northern New England, or upstate New York to play a round of golf. Gladly, these winter golfers abandon their snow-covered homes, and often they come in caravans across the Sagamore and Bourne bridges for one more round.

For such people, a good number of these courses have set a welcome mat not far from their 1st tees. At the gateway to the Cape & Islands in Wareham Bay Pointe Country Club sits beside Onset Bay, where snowstorms oft-times turn into rain. Bay Pointe's sandy-based fairways are usually the first to drain after heavy storms, and the first to reopen. Not far away, Little Harbor offers an enjoyable round of par-3 golf throughout the year in Wareham.

Weather permitting, Round Hill in Sandwich remains open just down Route 6, and winter becomes the only time of the year that non-members can play The Country Club of New Seabury in Mashpee.

In the mid-Cape area, Hyannis Golf Club holds weekly tournaments as long as there is no snow covering its fairways and greens, and Bass River remains open all winter, as well.

Out in the confines of the National Seashore, the pro shop at Highland Golf Links closes in November, but golfers work on the honor system to play out there long after that. They put $10 in a deposit box next to the clubhouse, then play all day. If the wind is blowing too strong across the highlands of North Truro, however, many of those same golfers head back to Chequessett, on the bay side of Wellfleet, where trees protect the course from mean off-shore winds.

No longer just a seasonal game for the wealthy on retreat, golf on Cape Cod, Nantucket & Martha's Vineyard is the nearest thing there is to a year-round sport. On the calendar, the season traditionally opens with the March of Dimes Tournament in March, before April's annual Seagulls Tournament opens at Hyannisport, usually in horrendous weather conditions. As the season quickly progresses, there are several other top notch tournaments: the Canal Classic and the annual television taping of the *Tucker Anthony Classic*, as well as the American Junior Golf Association Championship at New Seabury. In addition, there is the Cape Cod Junior Championship, the State Mid-Amateur, the Cape Cod Open, and the Cape Cod Amateur. By the calendar's end in December, the season concludes with the Cape Cod Pro-Am League.

With an oversubscribed membership of more than four hundred golfers, this Pro-Am League has become an institution on Cape Cod as its members play a different course every Wednesday in the spring and in the fall. This league began in the spring of 1950, when it was quiet at Hyannisport, and head professional George Morrison invited a group of his peers, as well as some of the top amateurs over for an informal tournament.

During that spring, other professionals in the area reciprocated at their clubs. As word spread about how wonderful the competition had proven to be, the fields of golfers grew. Come that fall, the informal group organized into the Cape Cod Pro-Am League, accepting by-laws and articles of organization.

From that meager beginning, the league has expanded so much that it is difficult to find a way into any one of their Wednesday tournament. The Pro-Am limits its fields to 144: two 4-man teams on each tee for a shotgun start. Players who were shutout one week, however, are automatically entered the succeeding week.

By 1984, the league finally needed an executive director to run all the events, so it signed James Gaquin, who is aided by his wife, Lois. Gaquin had spent more than thirty years working golf tournaments for both the Professional Golfers Association and the United States Golf Association, so he came well-qualified.

In addition to these fine events, the Cape & Islands have produced some outstanding players whose names have graced the rosters of the PGA and LPGA Tours.

Jim Hallet, for example, grew up a mile away from Bass River Golf Course and had plenty of rounds at the South Yarmouth course. And much the same is true with Sally Quinlan, who played at Dennis Pines as a young girl, before going on the LPGA tour from 1984 until 1990. Eventually, she left to become the golf coach at West Chester University in Pennsylvania. Not far behind her, Carri Wood, an aspiring LPGA Tour player, started in 1983 as a youngster picking up range balls at Blue Rock Golf Course. Although a Rhode Islander, Brad Faxon also can claim valid connections to the Cape. His family has long played at both Woods Hole in Falmouth and Eastward Ho! Country Club in Chatham. And Bill Buttner, who played on the PGA Tour from 1988 to 1992, learned his game at Plymouth.

Of all the local pros, though, the one golfer with the single greatest achievement to date is Henry Picard, who began as a caddie at Plymouth Country Club and won the Masters in 1938. Finishing second that year were Harry Cooper and Ralph Guldahl, while further back in the pack were Horton Smith, Byron Nelson and Gene Sarazen.

Beyond this game's rich local history, beyond this region's natural layout, and even beyond this area's collection of great courses with its own a roster of champions, golf on Cape Cod, Nantucket & Martha's Vineyard has become more than a thriving business. It has also become a source of revenue for charities throughout the Cape & Islands as some of this nation's best courses continue to play host to some of America's most celebrated golfers.

At Farm Neck, for example, President Clinton has played alongside such professional golfers as Billy Andrade and Betsy King at the annual fund-raiser for Martha's Vineyard Hospital, and former Red Sox outfielder Dom DiMaggio holds a tournament for the Dana Farber Foundation every June at his course, Kittansett. Willowbend's owner, Paul Fireman, continues to bring to the Cape a host of PGA Tour players, such as Greg Norman, John Daly, and Brad Faxon to raise money for a dozen different charities in the Mashpee area. And Chi Chi Rodriguez has held clinics at Ballymeade for youngsters from the Cape Cod chapter of Big Brothers and Big Sisters.

The biggest single celebrity tournament on the Cape and Islands, however, remains the Robert F. Kennedy Memorial Golf Tournament at The Hyannisport Club. The diverse field of golfers always includes celebrities, ranging from the likes of former Olympians Bruce Jenner and Rafer Johnson, and film stars Bill Murray and Randy Quaid, to former Chicago Bears great Gayle Sayers and Connecticut's Governor and former US Senator Lowell Weicker.

Clearly, the first 100 years of golf on Cape Cod, Nantucket & Martha's Vineyard have provided nothing less than a marvelous story; however, there is more to this story than the interest found in some passive tale. The fifty courses detailed in the following pages and their individual challenges guarantee an endless adventure, whose tale begins upon the 1st tee, whose cast includes hundreds of thousands of players, and whose enjoyment continues with every recollection of a round.

Notes

Section II

Ballymeade

1989: N. Falmouth/540-4005

Architects: Peter Dye, Brian Silva, Steve Harrison, Chi Chi Rodriguez, and Jim Fazio
Course Rating: 72.3 **Course Slope:** 137
Course Record: 4-under 68 by Ken Harrelson
Tee Time Policy: 7 days in advance
Amenities: Motor carts, alcohol bar, food service
The Skinny: Club is going private and limited public play is allowed.

Directions: From the Bourne Bridge, take Route 28 south to Route 151. Follow Route 151 east less than 1 mile to Falmouth Woods Road on your right, which is the entrance to Ballymeade. Should you find no tee times available here, not too much further along Route 151 you'll come across Cape Cod Country Club.

The Course

The story of Ballymeade is a somewhat crazy one. Stephen and Patricia Harrison, who began the Falmouth Woods project, went bankrupt, and then the government charged them with 100 counts of bank fraud in connection with more than twenty-eight million dollars worth of loans to build Ballymeade. But even from the very start, things were a bit bizarre.

Harrison had brought in Pete Dye as architect, and Dye prepared a preliminary routing plan. They couldn't agree, however, and soon parted company. Harrison then brought in Brian Silva, who did a more detailed plan before Harrison then discharged him. At that point, Harrison figured he could build the course by himself. And though his Ballymeade was indeed beautiful, it was also unplayable.

Now Ballymeade Country Club is coming back to life since a group of New England area

Hol	Par	Yds	Hcp
1	4	373	15
2	3	202	13
3	5	523	9
4	4	356	7
5	3	194	17
6	4	448	1
7	4	400	5
8	5	523	11
9	4	420	3
Out	36	3,439	
10	5	527	2
11	3	174	8
12	4	427	14
13	4	441	10
14	3	180	18
15	4	347	16
16	4	392	12
17	4	420	4
18	5	581	6
In	36	3,498	
Tot	72	6,928	

businessmen purchased the club in the spring of 1993. Though they plan to keep this a semi-private course for the near future, it won't remain open to the public for many years.

Until then, Ballymeade Development Corporation understands that the course requires some improvements if it is to become one of the premier courses in Massachusetts. So, they have hired PGA Senior Tour star Chi Chi Rodriguez, as well as golf architect Tom Fazio to revamp some of the trouble holes and make the course more playable. Fazio is one of the top architects in the country. Some of his coast line courses rank with the world's best, such as Wild Dunes outside of Charleston, South Carolina.

Meanwhile, the Arnold Palmer Golf Management Company of Orlando, Florida, is operating the facility, and memberships are available. "Arnold Palmer is the best name in golf, and his management group is the best in the industry," notes Peter Simonelli, vice president of golf operations. "They are service oriented. That fits with our direction."

9th HOLE

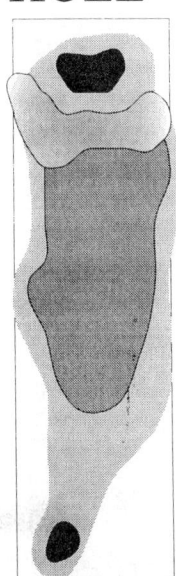

The Challenge

The old 9th had been a beautiful, dogleft right where you hit off an elevated tee; however, the contour of the fairway was to the left. Often drives would bounce sideways instead of forward. That made for long approach shots – more than 220 yards – to a green fronted by a protecting pond. And, yes, many balls wound up in the water.

The new owners knew that they had to make this hole more playable. Architect Jim Fazio built a new tee, then widened and leveled the fairway. Now when you hit a drive, your ball rolls forward instead of sideways, and you can hit an iron to the green.

It is best to hit your drive to the left side of the fairway, because that will open up the green for your second shot.

Bass River

1900: S. Yarmouth/398-9079

Architect: James Shepard, (expanded) Donald Ross
Course Rating: 68.4 **Course Slope:** 124
Course Record: 8-under 64 by George Nickerson (1962) and Don Brigham (1974)
Tee Time Policy: Four days in advance
Amenities: Motor carts & pull carts, alcohol bar, food service
The Skinny: There's such a great variety of holes, you'll find everything here.
Directions: From the Sagamore Bridge, take Route 6 east to Exit 8. Turn off the exit onto Station Avenue. After 2 miles, you will pass Dennis-Yarmouth High School on your left, then take the first left after the school onto Regional Avenue. At your second stop sign, you will see a fairway just ahead. Turn right onto High Bank Road, and the entrance will be about ¼ of a mile on your left.

The Course

With more than 85,000 rounds played on this course during some years, Bass River Golf Course is one of the busiest on the Cape & Islands. Not only does the greens crew perform a fantastic job of grooming, but this course also has a good mix of holes. Bass River is neither terrifying to the beginner, nor boring for the accomplished player.

"Everyone can enjoy it," boasts Walter Hewins, who served as head professional at Bass River for more than thirty years. "It's fairly open and not a bad course to walk."

Measuring 5,700 yards, Bass River is not a long course; however, the greens are small and difficult to hit. Short hitters can bounce their approach shots forward onto the green.

Originally a private course led by William A. Donald, Bass River Golf Course was incorporated by eight investors in 1900. James Shepard designed

Hol	Par	Yds	Hcp
1	4	329	8
2	4	348	9
3	4	282	17
4	3	105	18
5	5	464	5
6	3	139	13
7	3	190	7
8	4	282	14
9	4	391	2
Out	36	2,530	
10	4	247	16
11	4	386	1
12	5	450	4
13	5	500	3
14	3	140	15
15	4	333	6
16	5	474	11
17	4	319	12
18	4	339	10
In	37	3,172	
Tot	72	5,702	

the original course. His 9-hole track was spread over 50 acres. The greens were surrounded by fences, because livestock freely roamed the adjacent 50 acres. Routinely, they would traverse the golf course alongside the golfers, so Bass River fenced in the greens to prevent any damage from the cattle and goats.

In the 1920s Charles Henry Davis not only purchased the course from Donald and his investors, but also bought the adjoining land. That gave him a little more than 100 acres for a golf course, and he hired famed architect Donald Ross to expand Bass River to 18 holes for the owner and his friends.

When Davis died in the early 1950s, the town of Yarmouth purchased the course from his estate for $85,000. In addition to building a new clubhouse, the town changed a few of the holes. The 1st and the 8th were reconstructed during this realignment of holes.

In 1958, Bass River became public, and it remains an open course of small greens with four holes (the 3rd, 4th, 5th and 6th) bordering the Bass River that lends the course its name.

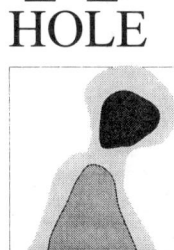

11th HOLE — *The Challenge*

From the blue markers, this par-4 measures 406 yards. You need to drive uphill through a narrow, tree-lined opening to a plateau, while a fairway bunker bears your watching on the left.

A good tee shot will leave you on the plateau of a high hill, looking down toward the green. Depending on the wind, your next shot could require a 3-wood or a 7-iron.

"You can bounce the ball on to many of the greens at Bass River; however, not on this hole," cautioned former head professional Walter Hewins.

If you come up short with your approach shot, your ball will hit the bank and roll down the hill into a depressed area. That would leave you with a difficult pitch shot straight up the hill.

The green is not very dangerous and there are no bunkers protecting it, either.

Bayberry Hills

1988: W. Yarmouth/394-5597

Architect: Brian Silva, Geoffrey Cornish
Course Rating: 68.5 **Course Slope:** 125
Course Record: 3-under 69 by Jim Hallet
Tee Time Policy: Four days in advance
Amenities: Motor carts & pull carts, alcohol bar, food service
Skinny: Nice course, but take a cart. Too long a walk between holes.

Directions: From the Sagamore Bridge, take Route 6 east to Exit 8. Turn right from the exit onto Station Avenue. At your second set of lights, turn right onto Old Townhouse Road. Follow this about 1 mile to its very end at West Yarmouth Road. There you will see the entrance to Bayberry Hills parking just ahead.

The Course

Built by the town of Yarmouth during the boom of the 1980s, Bayberry Hills is the sister course of Bass River, which was being overrun with golfers at the time.

"The real estate business was going crazy in the 80s," explains Walt Hewins, the former head professional at Bass River. "We figured it was now or never. If we didn't built a second course then, we would never have the opportunity nor land to build a second course."

The town paid more than one and a half million dollars for the land, then another two million for the construction of the golf course and facilities. Yarmouth hired architect Brian Silva, who had built both The Captains Course and Ocean Edge two towns over in Brewster. His final design has bent grass greens, fairways, and tees, as well as panoramic views from its hilly terrain.

Hol	Par	Yds	Hcp
1	4	375	3
2	5	485	9
3	3	140	17
4	4	336	7
5	4	335	15
6	4	350	13
7	5	505	1
8	3	146	11
9	4	350	5
Out	36	3,022	
10	4	372	4
11	4	384	2
12	3	130	18
13	4	320	16
14	4	352	8
15	5	503	10
16	4	349	6
17	3	160	14
18	5	475	12
In	36	3,045	
Tot	72	6,067	

While Bass River remains open year round, the town of Yarmouth closes Bayberry during the winter months. This gives it a chance to mature into a championship layout. At 7,000 yards from the back tees, Bayberry is one of the longest courses anywhere on Cape Cod, Nantucket & Martha's Vineyard.

"I like this course, because you can use your driver," says Ron Hewins, Bayberry Hills' head professional. "I hate courses where you have to keep laying up with irons on par-4s and par-5s."

Here you can take the driver out of your bag and hit away. It's a well-designed course.

"Another plus," he says, "is there aren't any blind shots, except maybe the approach shot to the 9th green. That's unique."

Depending on how you look at it, Bayberry can claim either another plus, or a major minus, for there is a healthy walk from one green to the next tee on a lot of holes.

"That acts as a buffer," explains Hewins. "The architect spaced the holes on a lot of land, and each hole is unique in itself. You're not hitting out of the next fairway if you miss a shot."

9th HOLE

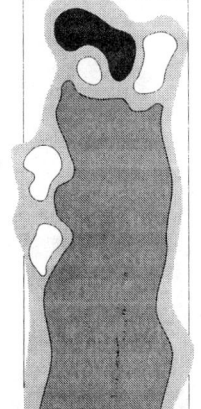

The Challenge

The 9th hole is not the most difficult according to the scorecard, where it ranks as the third most difficult hole on the front 9.

"No matter," says Ron Hewins, "it is a great hole."

The 9th is a par-4 of 350 yards from the members' tees. You hit out of a chute, and it favors anyone who can draw the ball a little. There isn't much of a landing area if you play your tee shot from the left to the right, and there are also 2 fairway bunkers.

Elevated and well-protected, the green has a cavernous bunker in the front with another to the left. And even once you're on it, this green has 2 tiers and remains difficult to putt. A lot of 3-putting goes on there.

The most difficult pin placement is back left. If the pin is there, you will cherish a par.

Bay Pointe

1965: Wareham/759-8802

Architect: Geoffrey Cornish
Course Rating: 69.1   **Course Slope:** 121
Course Record: 7-under 64 by Brian O'Hearn (1988)
Tee Time Policy: Seven days in advance
Amenities: Motor carts & pull carts, alcohol bar, food service
The Skinny: Some funky holes. The 17th is a peach.
Directions: From the Sagamore Bridge, take Route 6 west through Buzzards Bay and cross the highway bridge into Wareham. At the first set of lights, turn left onto Onset Avenue, which leads across a railroad bridge toward Onset. Bay Pointe is approximately 3 miles further on left.

The Course

After Wareham's Otis Phillips hired Geoffrey Cornish to design him a golf course on the hills above Onset Bay in 1964, Wareham Country Club opened in 1965. There were only twenty-seven courses in the greater Cape & Islands area back then, and golfers regarded this as one of the best; however, Wareham Country Club struggled for survival in the years before the second golf boom.

In 1978, the town of Wareham took over from Phillips and maintained it as a public golf course for the next nine years.

The town then sold the facility in 1987 to the Four Pines/Bay Pointe Corporation of Lexington, Massachusetts, who promised to build a hotel and a convention site, as well as to enhance the golf course. Though they changed the name of the course to Bay Pointe, a stagnant housing market forced them to file for bankruptcy. Rusty and

Hol	Par	Yds	Hcp
1	3	190	10
2	4	369	2
3	3	186	12
4	4	338	14
5	3	183	16
6	5	502	6
7	4	291	18
8	5	469	8
9	4	390	4
Out	35	3,102	
10	5	467	5
11	4	422	1
12	4	371	7
13	4	274	13
14	3	177	15
15	4	434	3
16	4	261	17
17	3	197	11
18	5	499	9
In	36	3,099	
Tot	72	6,201	

Robert Gunnarson of Duxbury headed a group of investors who purchased the course in 1993.

Long considered the gateway to the Cape & Islands, Bay Pointe remains open throughout the year. Its sandy-based soil usually is the first to drain from heavy storms, so the course reopens quickly. Golfers from snow-covered Northern New England hit here first as they look for fairways in late February and early March.

Over the years, there have been a few changes. The 12th has been changed somewhat with the addition of condominiums. They replaced the downhill and drivable par-4 13th hole. Bay Pointe added a new 17th hole with an island green.

Finally, let it be known that Bay Pointe's 10th, 11th, 12th holes are a local version of "Amen Corner." They are tough and unforgiving. And while the front 9 isn't a bad walk, the back 9 will leave you gasping.

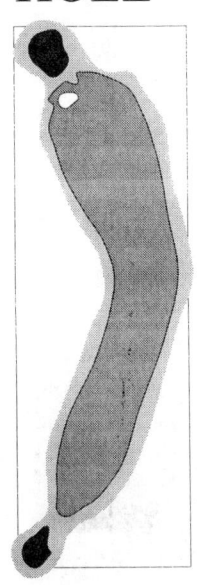

11th HOLE

The Challenge

There are two reasons why a golfer new to Bay Pointe is not frightened on the 11th tee. One reason is that the 11th hole seems playable, because you have just come off the terrifying 10th. The other is that this hole plays downhill from the tee, and you can't see the trouble. And there is plenty of it.

The 11th is the middle leg in an Unholy Trinity of holes that may well be the most difficult stretch anywhere on Cape Cod, Nantucket & Martha's Vineyard. This one is a sharp dogleg left par-4. Even the good players at the club have trouble reaching the green.

From the back tees it plays 422 yards and is the No. 1 stroke hole. You hit from an elevated tee down a sloping fairway; even if you place your drive in prime landing area, you still have an uphill shot of 190 yards.

The green is small and flat.

• 65 •

Blue Rock

1962: S. Yarmouth/398-9295

Architect: Geoffrey Cornish, William G. Robinson
Course Rating: N/A **Course Slope:** N/A
Course Record: 5-under 49 by five golfers, including Bob Miller, Ray Mello, and Paul Barkhouse
Tee Time Policy: Seven days in advance
Amenities: Rental clubs, pull carts, alcohol bar, food service
The Skinny: You may never, *ever* play a better par-3 course than Blue Rock.
Directions: From the Sagamore Bridge, take Route 6 east to Exit 8. Turn right off the ramp onto Station Avenue. At the first traffic light, turn left onto White's Path and follow this road about 1½ miles to its end.

Before you turn right onto Great Western Road, prepare to approach an odd intersection. Though the road curves to the left, you are actually staying straight onto Great Western Road. The entrance to Blue Rock is about ¼ of a mile further on the right.

The Course

Legend has it that explorer Leif Erickson sailed up the Bass River, anchored his ship, and stepped out onto a blue rock. A lot happened after that, but the Viking eventually got back in his boat, turned around, and headed home.

"I've been out on the river in my boat, and there truly is a huge boulder under the water," claims Bob Miller head professional at the course which takes its name from that legend. "If the water is still, you can see that the rock actually has a blue tinge to it."

Long after the Norsemen left, the architectural team of Geoffrey Cornish and William Robinson started building this par-3 golf course in 1961. The first course on the Cape since the Great Depression, Blue Rock officially opened in June of 1962 with an all-star cast that included Francis Ouimet, Dave Marr, and Pat Berg, and it proved so popular that

Hol	Par	Yds	Hcp
1	3	103	17
2	3	127	15
3	3	118	13
4	3	125	11
5	3	247	1
6	3	145	9
7	3	170	5
8	3	165	7
9	3	165	3
Out	27	1,365	
10	3	150	10
11	3	117	18
12	3	190	2
13	3	147	12
14	3	185	6
15	3	185	8
16	3	144	14
17	3	144	16
18	3	173	4
In	27	1,381	
Tot	54	2,746	

others were enticed to consider building still more courses on the Cape and Islands.

Ever since, several other great players have walked the fairways and greens of Blue Rock, including Betsy King, Beth Daniel, and Pat Bradley, all of whom played in Sally Quinlan's Brookside Hospital Golf Tournament. In fact, it was here that both Quinlan and LPGA aspirant Carri Wood learned quite a bit about the game from Bob Miller, one of the pioneers in Cape & Islands golf schools ever since he started his own at Blue Rock in 1978. In addition, Miller has brought Blue Rock many other tournaments.

Sports Illustrated has rated Blue Rock as one of the finest par-3s in the country, and you need all the clubs in your bag to get around these 18 holes with any degree of success. They range from the 1st hole of just over 100 yards to the mammoth 5th hole of just under 250. In the first thirty years of its existence, Blue Rock has allowed only three aces on its longest hole. Tom Martin, Bob Baker and Norm Babineau are the only ones *ever* to card a 1 on it.

9th HOLE

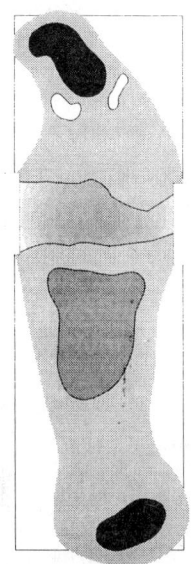

The Challenge

When you stand on the elevated 9th tee, you see an angled, kidney-shaped green that seems difficult to hit. There is a pond you must drive across, and there are 2 big bunkers fronting the green. A saving grace is that the green is moderately flat; however, getting to the green is the problem, and therein lies the challenge that makes this Blue Rock's signature hole.

From the back markers, it is 170 yards from the tee to the middle. If you hit a fade shot, the green seems smaller and that will make this tee shot even more nerve-wracking. So, this hole proves better suited to a draw shot. Head pro Bob Miller says that players have hit anything from a mid-iron to a fairway wood.

Just hope that the pin is not in the back left, otherwise it will make it just that much more difficult.

ନ୍ତ *The Complete Guide to Golf*

Cape Cod

1929: N. Falmouth/563-9842

Architect: Devereaux Emmet, Alfred Tull
Course Rating: 70.0   **Course Slope:** 120
Course Record: 7-under 64 by Jeff Lewis (1979)
Tee Time Policy: One week in advance
Amenities: Motor carts & pull carts, alcohol bar, food service
The Skinny: This is a place that players of any skill level will enjoy.

Directions: From the Bourne Bridge, take Route 28 south to Route 151. Take Route 151 east, where you will pass Ballymeade on your right before you come to Cape Cod Country Club about 2 miles further along on your right.

Even further along in this direction are Paul Harney's, Falmouth Country Club, and Quashnet Valley.

The Course

In 1929, Cape Cod Country Club opened as a 9-holer called Coonamesset, because of the nearby inn of the same name. Designed by Devereaux Emmet and Al Tull, who had created Wee Burn Country Club in Connecticut, as well as the old Congressional Country Club outside of D.C., the course is rumored to have been redesigned and expanded to 18 holes not long thereafter by noted architect Donald Ross; however, head pro Chuck Holmes has looked everywhere and cannot find any proof that Ross ever set foot on these fairways.

"It would be nice to say this is a Donald Ross course," he admits, "but we have no real evidence."

Meanwhile, Coonamesset underwent several name changes: it then spent two years as the Treadway Inn during the 1950s before it became Clausen's in the 1960s. In 1977, the course became the Cape Cod Country Club.

Hol	Par	Yds	Hcp
1	4	325	15
2	3	207	7
3	5	495	11
4	4	425	3
5	4	440	1
6	5	520	9
7	4	315	17
8	4	417	5
9	3	165	13
Out	36	3,299	
10	4	420	4
11	5	515	6
12	3	265	10
13	5	461	8
14	4	365	2
15	3	190	12
16	3	205	16
17	4	310	18
18	4	325	14
In	35	3,095	
Tot	71	6,404	

• 68 •

In the 1950s, three consecutive Massachusetts State Opens were held here: John Thoren won the title in 1955; Ed Oliver, in 1956; and Bob Crowley won the first of his four State Opens in 1957.

In 1985, Phil Friel, who owns and leases several golf courses in New Hampshire, purchased Cape Cod Country Club, and since then he has made a steady stream of improvements to the course.

The beauty of Cape Cod Country Club is that it sets up for every one. The good players can go to the blue tees, and it will play difficult for them. The average golfer can play from the white tees and enjoy themselves, too. Meanwhile, there are tricky putting surfaces, such as the 6th green and the 18th. The latter is a short hole, but the green makes up for it. Perhaps the prettiest hole is the 9th, a short par-3 over a pond with another huge pond to the left.

"It's probably the hilliest course that doesn't play hilly," claims Holmes. "There are plenty of hills, but they are all on tees and greens," he further explains. "For a hilly course, you have plenty of flat lies."

8th HOLE

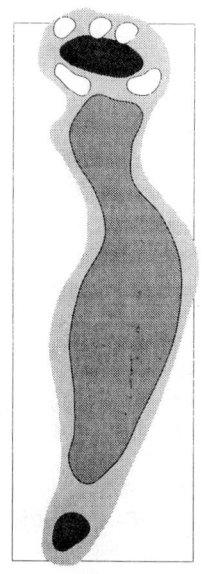

The Challenge

"This is a brutal hole," says head professional Chuck Holmes. It's a par-4 measuring more than 400 yards from the members' tee.

The hole begins out of a chute, so you have to hit it straight and hope your ball will land on a plateau out there. "The second shot used to be too difficult," admits Holmes. "There was a swamp instead of fairway, so if you missed your second shot, you would lose a ball in the muck."

Though the greens crew has since dried out the swamp and created a fairway, that has not made this hole drastically easier. It has simply made it less difficult to lose as many balls.

You still have to hit the green, and that isn't easy either. Upon an elevated shelf and protected by bunkers to the left and right, the green has 3 more small bunkers behind it to catch any balls that might be headed toward an otherwise watery grave.

Captains

1985: Brewster/896-5100

Architect: Brian Silva
Course Rating: 72.0 **Course Slope:** 130
Course Record: 4-under 68 by Jim Hallet (blue tees), 5-under 67 Peter Courville (white tees)
Tee Time Policy: Two days (longer if prepaid)
Amenities: Motor carts & pull carts, alcohol bar, food service
The Skinny: A real treat. The best bunch of par-3s in the entire state.
Directions: From the Sagamore Bridge, take Route 6 east to Exit 11. From the ramp turn right onto Route 137, cross over Route 6, and follow Long Pond Road for 1½ miles. Turn right onto South Orleans Road/Freemans Way follow this another 1½ miles. Just after you cross back over Route 6, you will find The Captains is on your right.

The Course

From its name to its layout, The Captains is unique among courses on Cape Cod, Nantucket & Martha's Vineyard. When the town fathers got around to deciding what to call the golf course, they wanted a distinguishable name. With all good intentions, then, they planned to honor one of the old sea captains who had made Brewster prominent during the 19th century.

Deciding upon which particular captain to honor, however, fast became a problem. So, after checking with the historical society, the town decided to name each of the 18 holes after eighteen different sea captains. All of which proved to be just one more in a series of wise decisions.

From the start, The Captains has been a success, not only for its impeccable conditions, but also for its shot value and esthetics. It is the first public course on Cape Cod with bentgrass tees,

Hol	Par	Yds	Hcp
1	4	350	10
2	4	378	2
3	3	157	18
4	5	478	8
5	4	328	12
6	5	501	4
7	4	344	6
8	3	182	14
9	4	317	16
Out	36	2,965	
10	4	321	11
11	3	127	17
12	4	370	5
13	4	426	1
14	5	531	3
15	4	331	9
16	4	354	13
17	3	171	15
18	5	575	7
In	35	3,205	
Tot	72	6,170	

fairways, and greens. There are 7 acres of Penncross creeping bentgrass on tees and greens, plus another 26 acres on the fairways.

Although Brian Silva consulted with his partner, Geoffrey Cornish, through every phase of its development, this course was his first solo design. *Golf Digest* judged this Brewster layout as the Best New Public Course in the country in 1985, the *only* New England course ever to receive such an honor.

Beyond the praise, there remain countless other wonderful facets of The Captains. The 3rd and 11th holes, for example, are beautiful par-3s with elevated tees that overlook generously bunkered greens. The par-4 12th teases with an uneven fairway, and the 9th hole has a devilish fairway bunker to the right. The 7th hole, a short dogleg right, dares you to try to drive over the trees onto a multi-leveled green. And there is only one water hole on the course, the par-5 14th, where you have to carry the water to reach the green.

2nd HOLE

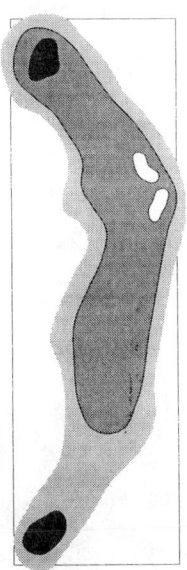

The Challenge

The 2nd hole may not be the most dramatic at The Captains, but it exemplifies what makes a good golf hole a *good golf* hole; namely, shot value.

A dogleg to the left, this is the most difficult hole on the front 9; however, it is only 375 yards from the middle tees. "You can't just go to the tee and try to bang the ball out there," says Brian Silva. "Thought has to go into the shot."

Every hole should have one special shot, and this one is no different. If you execute it properly, your reward will be an easier second shot. Silva warns against trying to cut the dogleg. Even if you hit to the middle of the fairway, you'll have a tough shot over trees guarding the green. The key here is to aim at the opposite side of the dogleg, directly at the fairway bunkers that seem almost reachable. If you hit your drive away from the dogleg, you will have a clear second shot to the green.

Chequessett

1929: Wellfleet/349-3704

Architect: L.D. Baker
Course Rating: 64.1 **Course Slope:** 111
Course Record: 6-under 64 by Mike Flanagan
Tee Time Policy: Five days in advance
Amenities: Motor carts & pull carts, alcohol bar, food service
The Skinny: Some interesting holes for a short course.
Directions: From the Sagamore Bridge, take Route 6 east to Wellfleet Center signs and turn left onto Main Street toward the center. Shortly after entering onto Main Street, take a left onto East Commercial Street, which leads you toward Town Pier. At the waterfront, turn right onto Beach Road and follow this about 1 mile further to Chequessett on the right.

The Course

A fun 9-holer (par 35) located alongside Cape Cod Bay in Wellfleet, Chequessett is a course in transition. The late Lorenzo Dow Baker (whose family had founded the United Fruit Company) built the golf course in 1929 as another source of recreation for his Chequessett Yacht Club. Back then, the price of the land was right: just $62 an acre. Today, an acre of Wellfleet land can go for more than $100,000.

At just over 5,000 yards from the men's tees, this isn't a long course. Still, nobody seems capable of bringing it to its knees. One reason is the wind, which wreaks havoc as golfers attempt to hit accurate approach shots to its dime-size greens. Another reason is the number of *burns* meandering throughout Chequessset. *Burns* is a Scottish term for ditches that crisscross several fairways.

The course has had several alterations over the

Hol	Par	Yds	Hcp
1	4	235	13
2	3	132	15
3	4	132	3
4	5	431	7
5	3	109	17
6	4	299	9
7	4	363	1
8	4	369	5
9	4	278	11
Out	35	2,561	
10	4	235	18
11	3	153	14
12	4	342	8
13	5	444	10
14	3	168	6
15	4	243	16
16	4	363	2
17	4	377	4
18	4	263	12
In	35	2,588	
Tot	70	5,162	

years. The club shortened the 1st hole when tennis courts were added to the facility. There may be more changes in the coming years. Sherwood A. Moore, the former superintendent of Winged Foot GC in Mamaroneck, New York, has consulted with officials about changing a few holes.

Meanwhile, another improvement to Chequessett has been the installation of an irrigation system, and the improvement has been noticeable. Usually burnt-out by summer, for example, the first four fairways were an exercise in frustration before the implementation of the irrigation system. You could not play the ball down because of ruddy and uneven lies.

Still, the greens remain tricky. "They are old," admits Dick Sjorgen, "and there are about four types of grasses mixed together."

A Worcester native who retired to Cape Cod, Sjorgen is a former member of Pleasant Valley Country Club, who saw a notice that the club needed someone for two days a week. Soon after, he began working five days a week, and the following year became club manager in 1992.

3rd HOLE

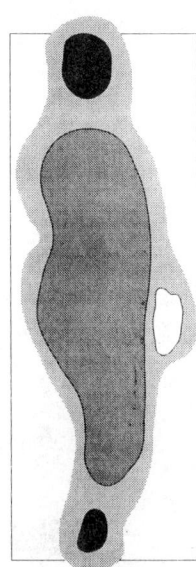

The Challenge

From this green, you see Wellfleet Harbor and Cape Cod Bay, making the 3rd hole one of the most picturesque at Chequessett. Still, you must work your way toward that reward.

You hit from an elevated tee, and the fairway rises with the green atop another hill. If you miss your drive, you could wind up in a burn. If you fade, you could land in a devious sand bunker on the right. If you are any further off line, your ball could nestle in the underbrush bordering the hole.

Even if your drive is true, you will have a tricky approach shot. If you are at the bottom of the fairway, it could be a blind shot without any target to aim for. Instead, it is all guess work.

Beyond all that, the green is hazard free. When they built the green, they carved it out of the top of the hill. It is as minimalist and as natural as any green you will play.

Cotuit Highground

1929: Cotuit/428-9863

Architect: Unknown
Course Rating: None **Course Slope:** None
Course Record: 5-under 49 by Ed Savery
Tee Time Policy: One day in advance
Amenities: Pull carts, pro shop
The Skinny: Not that tough a course to walk.
Directions: From the Sagamore Bridge, take Route 6 east to Exit 2. From the ramp, turn right onto Route 130 south and follow this through Sandwich and Mashpee to its very end at Route 28 in Barnstable. Turn left onto Route 28, then take your very first right onto Main Street that leads through Cotuit Center. Follow this for nearly 2 miles and watch for School Street on your right. Turn onto School Street for about ½ mile, then take your second left onto Crocker Neck Road. The course is just down the road.

Meanwhile, you might want to drive about another 2 miles further along this quaint, winding road to get a look at The Willowbend Club, which is just over the Barnstable town line in Mashpee.

The Course

Cotuit Highground has been around ever since Calvin Coolidge was President. The Fowler family of Falmouth built this course in the Barnstable village of Cotuit back in 1929, then operated it until World War II, when the course was closed for the war's duration. Come the end of that war, the course reopened. In 1954, John Heher purchased this 9-hole layout, and the Hehers have overseen Cotuit Highground ever since.

In the best sense of the term, this is simply a "Mom & Pop" operation. Cotuit belongs to neither the Massachusetts Golf Association, nor the United States Golf Association, and there is no PGA head pro on hand. And though this is not a championship course, its narrow, hilly fairways and crowned greens offer a definite challenge.

All things considered, Cotuit Highground is a place for fun with a local membership, mostly of

Hol	Par	Yds	Hcp
1	3	115	14
2	3	180	4
3	4	290	6
4	3	130	12
5	3	140	8
6	3	110	16
7	3	100	18
8	3	180	2
9	3	115	10
Out	28	2,325	
10	3	115	10
11	3	180	11
12	4	290	5
13	3	130	13
14	3	140	9
15	3	110	15
16	3	100	17
17	3	180	1
18	3	115	9
In	28	2,325	
Tot	54	4,650	

golfers from Barnstable and Falmouth. "We have a lot of beginners and a lot of youngsters," adds Heher, who provides several clinics for the kids. If you want to play, it is better to come on a weekday; on weekend mornings during the season there are club tournaments. Still, some times are available on Saturday and Sunday afternoons.

Its size and casual atmosphere aside, Cotuit Highground still has enjoyed its share of interesting happenings. Take, for example, the tournament back in the 1960s when two golfers made *back-to-back* holes-in-one on the 150-yard 5th hole. Ironically, neither golfer enjoyed the immediate excitement of his feat, for it's a blind shot.

The late Tony Souza was the first one to get an ace, witnessed by somebody on the next tee who looked over and saw the ball drop into the cup. Then, as the entire foursome on the 6th tee was still watching, Peter Ansewitz followed after Souza. His ball gently hit the green and rolled into the hole on top of Souza's ball.

The odds of a hole-in-one are 35,000:1. The odds of successive shots going into the cup are incalculable.

8th HOLE

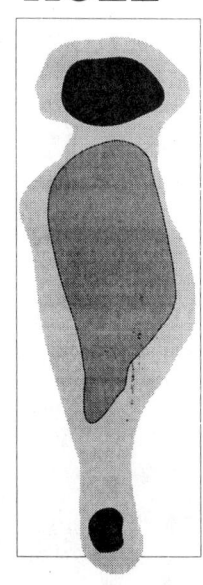

The Challenge

You usually think of par-3 holes as easy; however, the 8th hole at Cotuit Highground is the toughest on the course. A par is a great score on this hole, but most golfers walk away with a bogey or worse.

"You need to have an accurate tee shot if you want to make par here," says John Heher. Most players hit either a long iron, or a fairway wood.

The 8th measures 180 yards, and there are no bunkers to fret about; however, the fairway is narrow. More importantly, though, the trouble is the green. It is, as Heher calls it, "shaped like a turtle's back."

If you hit the green anywhere but the front center, you will have a difficult time holding the green. If you miss the green, you will have a difficult chip because of the crowned nature of the hole.

Cranberry Valley

1974: Brewster/430-7560

Architect: Geoffrey Cornish, William G. Robinson
Course Rating: 70.4 **Course Slope:** 123
Course Record: 5-under 67 by Peter Morgan
Tee Time Policy: Two days in advance (longer, if prepaid)
Amenities: Motor carts & pull carts, food service
The Skinny: This is one of the truly *must* courses on the Cape.

Directions: From the Sagamore Bridge, take Route 6 east to Exit 10. From the exit, turn right onto Route 124 south. Take your second left onto Queen Ann Road and follow about ½ mile to Oak Street on your right. Turn onto Oak Street and you will find Cranberry Valley on your left.

The Course

For several years, *Golf Digest* ranked Cranberry Valley Golf Course among the Top 75 Public Golf Courses in America. Though it belongs on that list for its entire existence, Cranberry Valley dropped in the ranks in recent years through no fault of its own. This course has never fallen into any state of disrepair; on the contrary, it is *always* in superb condition. The simple reason for the slip off the list is the proliferation of new, high-end public courses that have been entering the market. Cranberry Valley, though, can stand on its merit. It *is* a great public course.

One reason is simply that there are no weak holes at Cranberry Valley. They wind through woods and marsh, as well as through its *nom de guerre:* cranberry bogs. The tees are uncommonly large for any course on Cape Cod, Nantucket & Martha's Vineyard. The greens are also bigger than

Hol	Par	Yds	Hcp
1	4	357	9
2	5	473	11
3	4	473	3
4	3	188	15
5	4	424	1
6	4	323	13
7	3	164	17
8	5	502	7
9	4	378	5
Out	36	3,191	
10	4	350	6
11	4	345	14
12	4	361	8
13	3	165	18
14	5	439	12
15	4	303	16
16	4	438	2
17	3	211	10
18	5	493	4
In	36	3,105	
Tot	72	6,296	

the average seacoast course, but they are not easy to hit. The ever-present and shifting breezes, together with bunkers strategically placed throughout the course remain a constant worry for your approach to the green. Greenside bunkers, however, are not the only ones to worry about, for there are 14 fairway bunkers, too. In addition, the layout provides 7 doglegs, including a *double* dogleg par-5 on the 18th to make it one of the greatest finishing holes anywhere on the Cape & Islands.

Aside from their strength, there also are no easy holes at Cranberry Valley, where even the par-3s are heroic. The shortest is 165 yards from the middle tees, and most of them require a long iron or fairway wood. The two shorter par-3s are well-bunkered to prevent any fortuitous bounces.

Beyond the skill factor, Cranberry Valley provides plenty of vivid views. From the clubhouse you can look down the narrow, winding 10th fairway. In front of the large green is a pond that seems so tranquil. Yet, you know a few mental breakdowns have begun with some errant shots into the water hazard.

5th HOLE

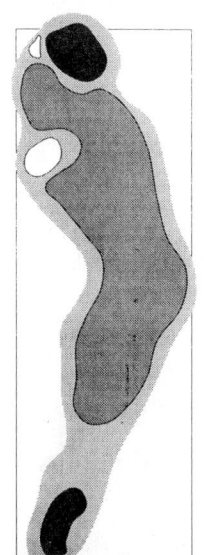

The Challenge

If you walk away from the 5th hole at Cranberry Valley with a par, you should be a happy camper. The toughest hole on the course, this is a par-4 of 424 yards from the middle tees that bends to the left. Of the 18 challenging holes, the 5th is undoubtedly the No. 1 stroke hole.

You must drive your tee shot long enough to get beyond the dogleg. If you can't do that, you will not have a clear approach to the green. The approach shot then demands a high shot that must not only carry a mound in front of the green, but also must avoid the large bunkers both in front and to the left of the putting surface.

Simply said, getting there is most of the trouble on this monster par-4.

Cummaquid

1895: Yarmouthport/362-2022

Architect: Unknown, (r) Henry Mitchell
Course Rating: 70.2 **Course Slope:** 126
Course Record: 7-under 64 by Jim Hallet, John Sances, Brian Stewart, and Jeff Lewis
Tee Time Policy: Private course that must be played with a member
Amenities: Motor carts & pull carts, alcohol bar, food service

The Skinny: Delightful course that can jump up and become a beast.
Directions: From the Sagamore Bridge, take Route 6 east to Exit 7. From the exit, turn right onto Willow Street and drive about 2 miles north to Route 6A. Turn left onto Route 6A, and about ¼ mile on your left you will find the entrance to Cummaquid just across the Barnstable line.

The Course

Cummaquid Golf Club revels in its distinction as the oldest golf *club* on Cape Cod, Nantucket & Martha's Vineyard. The club founders played the game informally on the Cape as early as 1893, when they used the farmlands of Henry Thacher and Dr. Gorham Bacon in Yarmouthport and Barnstable.

The Cummaquid Golf Club of Barnstable and Yarmouthport organized on August 17, 1895, and by the following January it had completed its clubhouse: one large room with a fireplace, plus smaller dressing rooms for the men and women.

Among its first members was John Reed, who vacationed in Hyannisport. More familiar with golf than was any other member, Reed had been one of the founding fathers of St. Andrews Golf Club in Yonkers, New York, which is reputed to be *the* oldest golf club in America.

Hol	Par	Yds	Hcp
1	4	343	13
2	5	528	5
3	4	416	3
4	4	394	1
5	3	166	17
6	4	334	11
7	4	375	7
8	3	168	15
9	5	501	9
Out	36	3,225	
10	4	400	6
11	4	370	8
12	4	304	16
13	3	202	12
14	5	444	14
15	4	377	10
16	3	150	18
17	4	405	2
18	4	425	4
In	35	3,077	
Tot	71	6,302	

No one knows who built Cummaquid; however, it is believed that a committee of the club founders laid out and built a rudimentary 9-hole course on farmland with stonewalls crisscrossing fairways. Over the years, Cummaquid refined its 9-hole layout, and the stonewalls were done away with. Some stonewalls were buried, thus accounting for Cummaquid's rolling hills. Others were removed altogether, though, and their stones were sold for use in the foundation of nearby Route 6A.

In the late 1960s, Cummaquid hired architect Henry Mitchell to expand the course from 9 to 18 holes, and he combined some of the old holes with the new ones to create two new 9s.

During its long and fabled history, Cummaquid twice nearly disappeared into oblivion, both times after the World Wars. In 1918, only three members appeared at the annual meeting. In 1946, enough members attended that meeting to oppose any closing, thus restoring life to the old club. After the war, membership began to swell. By 1966, there were a record 146 members; by 1972, the number reached 290, forcing a long waiting list ever since.

17th HOLE *The Challenge*

Imagine that the match is coming down to the final two holes, and you are having a career round. This is *not* the time you should have to play the 17th at Cummaquid, the No. 2 stroke hole, as well as the toughest one on Cummaquid's back 9.

There is one pond in front of the tee, another to the right of the fairway and a third to the left. From the back tees, the hole plays just over 400 yards. The average golfer hits anywhere from a 4-iron to a 3-wood to an elevated green, and the prevailing wind blows from left to right. If you fade the ball, as most golfers do, it's exaggerated.

You have to hit straight off the tee. If you try to cut the corner on this dogleg right, you could get waterlogged. Meanwhile, a bunker protects the left side of the green. Finally, the putting surface is not too severe, your only reward for surviving the first phase of the hole.

Dennis Highlands

1985: Dennis/385-8347

Architect: Michael Hurdzan
Course Record: 4-under 67 by Keith Lewis (1986)
Course Rating: 70.4 **Course Slope:** 118
Tee Time Policy: Four days in advance (longer, if prepaid)
Amenities: Motor carts & pull carts, alcohol bar, food service
The Skinny: Always remember that you must stay awake on the putting surface.
Directions: From the Sagamore Bridge, take Route 6 east to Exit 9. From the exit, turn left onto Route 134 north. After you cross over Route 6, you will come to a set of traffic lights at the police station. Turn left onto Access Road and follow this about ¼ of a mile to its end. Turn right onto Old Bass River Road, where Dennis Highlands is about 2 miles further north on your left.

The Course

When Dennis Highlands opened in 1985, it was a simple case of bad timing. The Town of Dennis was launching this gem just as The Captains Course was opening in Brewster. While The Captains took the award for Best New Course of 1985 from *Golf Digest*, Dennis Highlands finished as a runner-up. Perhaps if it had opened either earlier or later, the story might have been different. None of that, though, should lessen the reputation of this course.

Built upon one of the hilliest pieces of glacial moraine in the middle of the peninsula, The Highlands *is* exactly what its name asserts. If you were lucky enough to play this course when it opened, however, you know that Dennis Highlands was much different then than it is now.

The architect who later built The Willowbend Club, Michael Hurdzan had cultivated tall fescue grasses on the perimeter of the rough. There are

Hol	Par	Yds	Hcp
1	4	324	16
2	5	524	4
3	3	177	15
4	4	354	14
5	4	362	8
6	7	416	1
7	3	187	12
8	5	492	6
9	3	157	18
Out	35	2,983	
10	4	390	9
11	3	178	17
12	4	394	10
13	4	409	7
14	4	403	11
15	5	563	3
16	3	219	13
17	4	384	5
18	5	541	2
In	36	3,481	
Tot	71	6,464	

some twelve different types of wildflower grasses planted in the high grass, so when the constant Cape winds blew, they lent the course a look of ocean waves. In addition, the bunkers originally had some peculiar sand: a grainy, bright white stock that made you squint when you looked at it. Before long, though, the high fescue was cut down, because it was taking golfers too long to find their errant shots. Then, the blinding sand was replaced.

Because this is not among the longest courses on the Cape & Islands, even the average golfer might reach all the greens in regulation; however, this requires a blend of controlled power, bold finesse and chess-like strategy. The layout has terraced tees and greens, as well as 42 bunkers strategically placed to menace only the best of players. Among them also are enough Scottish hummocks to distort the distance on many approach shots. Overall, you need to play each hole in your mind from the pin back to the tee. Given difficult pin placements, a good strategy is to position your drive with precision. That way you can have the most green to work with for your approach shots.

6th HOLE

The Challenge

If you are a long hitter, you have an advantage on this hole, a par-4 that plays just over 400 yards from the back tees and is all uphill.

For the average hitter, the landing area slopes to the right, and that takes away any forward roll you might otherwise get. If your drive fades to the right, the slope of the fairway could also send the shot bouncing into a waste area. Even if you manage to keep your tee shot in the fairway, your work has only begun to the two-tiered green some 50 to 70 feet above the fairway. There is a bunker to the left, as well as one behind the green. If you think you need a 5-iron, take at least one more club, perhaps two (or a fairway wood).

Then, if you are fortunate enough to reach the green in regulation, you should hope you are on the right level. If you are on the wrong plateau, you will be lucky to walk off the green with a 2-putt.

Dennis Pines

1965: Dennis/385-8698

Architect: Henry Mitchell
Course Rating: 71.9 **Course Slope:** 127
Course Record: 5-under 67 by Jay Haberl and Ed Kirby
Tee Time Policy: Four days advance (longer, if prepaid)
Amenities: Motor carts & pull carts, alcohol bar, food service

The Skinny: One of the most underrated courses on the Cape & Islands.
Directions: From the Sagamore Bridge, take Route 6 east to Exit 9. From the exit, turn left onto Route 134 and drive north back over Route 6 for about 2 miles. Dennis Pines will be on your right.

The Course

Dennis Pines is certainly one of the better – perhaps even *the* most underrated – town-owned courses in Massachusetts. Designed by architect Henry Mitchell in 1965, this is one of the oldest town-owned courses on Cape Cod, Nantucket & Martha's Vineyard. Aside from being older than its sister course, The Dennis Highlands, Dennis Pines is also longer and more difficult. In short, you need an accurate tee shot, as well as sharp irons to shoot a career round here.

The fairways are narrow and often balls will bounce into the tree line. So, be forewarned: when you play this gem of a course carved out of dense woods, be careful not to hit it off line. If you do, you might wish you had an axe in your bag to extricate yourself. In addition, the 10th and the 11th holes are beauties around a pond that most certainly catches errant drives.

Hol	Par	Yds	Hcp
1	4	400	9
2	4	432	7
3	5	505	11
4	3	192	17
5	5	518	13
6	4	447	5
7	3	203	15
8	4	470	1
9	4	403	3
Out	36	3,570	
10	4	380	8
11	4	412	10
12	5	537	2
13	3	207	16
14	4	433	4
15	5	502	14
16	4	365	12
17	3	205	18
18	4	418	6
In	36	3,459	
Tot	72	7,029	

The greens are comparatively larger than on most Cape & Islands courses; however, that does not mean that they are easier to hit. Sand bunkers and strategically placed trees protect The Pines' sprawling greens.

Unless I mention this, you might otherwise remain unaware that both Dennis Pines and Dennis Highlands share a unique rule that conflicts with those of the United States Golf Association. Despite that conflict, this rule makes sense. If you are in a bunker, and a stone interferes with your shot, you are allowed to remove the pebble. This rule applies also at The Kittansett Club in Marion, as well as at British and Scottish courses alike; however, the USGA does not allow such a move.

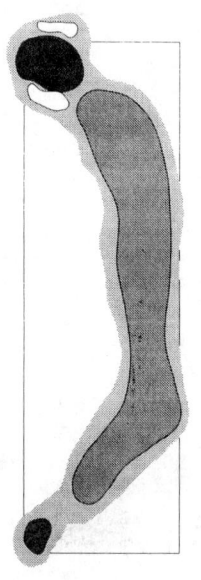

12th HOLE *The Challenge*

This hole seems to go on *forever*. So much so that, if you are having trouble hitting the ball, this will seem like the Bataan Death March. Perhaps one of the toughest par-5s on the Cape & Islands, the 12th is a *double* dogleg left stretching a long 537 yards from the back markers.

From the back tees, this green has been reached in 2 shots only by three players: amateur Kevin Carey, former Massachusetts Open winner Craig Madson, and Michael Haberl, son of The Dennis Pines' head pro.

Still, Jay Haberl notes that some of their good players don't even try to reach the green in 2. Instead, they tee off with an iron so they will be in position with their second shot. From there, he says, they hit a 3-wood and then a wedge.

The green is well-bunkered. The toughest pin placement is on the left behind a bunker.

Eastward Ho!

1923: Chathamport/945-0620

Architect: Herbert Fowler
Course Rating: 70.3 **Course Slope:** 130
Course Record: 5-under 67 by Charlie Birch
Tee Time Policy: Private course
Amenities: Motor carts, alcohol bar and food service
The Skinny: This is one course where the elements beat you *all* the time.
Directions: From the Sagamore Bridge, take Route 6 east to Exit 11. From the exit, turn left onto Route 137, then take an immediate first left onto Pleasant Bay Road. This road travels through Harwich for about 2 miles and crosses Route 39 before it ends at Route 28. At the end of Pleasant Bay Road, turn right on onto Route 28, where you will see Pleasant Bay and Round Cove on your left. Take your first onto Fox Hill Road, where you will find Eastward Ho! about ½ mile on your left.

The Course

In the days before Ross began designing golf courses, Britain's Herbert Fowler was probably the most gifted architect in the game, and he had designed two of the most famous courses in the United Kingdom: Walton Heath and Westward Ho! The Cape's Eastward Ho! is one of only six courses in America designed by Fowler, and this may be *the* best. It combines the rolling terrain and ocean setting of a links course, with the tree-lined fairways and elevated greens of a heathland course.

First conceived in 1912, but never begun in earnest until 1922, Eastward Ho! is certainly a jewel overlooking both Pleasant Bay and the Atlantic at Chathamport. The club's founders were a prestigious group that included G. Herbert Windeler, a member of The Country Club and former president of the USGA. Knowing what they wanted, they sought out several sites on Cape Cod

Hol	Par	Yds	Hcp
1	4	376	9
2	4	354	11
3	4	308	17
4	3	168	15
5	5	497	3
6	5	403	2
7	3	177	7
8	4	324	13
9	4	393	5
Out	36	3,002	
10	3	214	10
11	5	487	4
12	4	322	12
13	4	336	16
14	4	373	14
15	3	142	18
16	4	364	8
17	5	515	6
18	4	460	2
In	36	3,213	
Tot	72	6,215	

for a summer club before selecting this topography that has *everything* a golf course architect looks for: sand, turf, elevation, wind, and a majestic view.

Fowler's fairways grass was imported from New Zealand; his greens, from Central Europe. When he finally completed Eastward Ho!, he left nothing to chance. After Francis Ouimet, the 1913 US Open champion, managed only an uncharacteristic 87 in the 1923 opening, Ouimet called it the most difficult course he *ever* played.

Indeed, Fowler had designed every hole to bring out the best a golfer can hope for. The first 9 holes stretch toward the east and the Atlantic Ocean; the incoming 9 run along the shores of Pleasant Bay. There are no blind shots, and there are no adjacent fairways. You cannot afford to fall asleep during a round. You must think on every shot you take.

Because of its particular location, the weather on this course might change suddenly, or else it might be drastically different just a short distance away.

18th HOLE

The Challenge

This may be *the* best finishing hole anywhere on Cape Cod, Nantucket & Martha's Vineyard. So good is this 460-yard par-4 that even scratch players are ecstatic with a par.

If the wind is out of the east, you will be playing directly into it from an elevated tee with Pleasant Bay to your left. The fairway drops to a landing area that is not visible from the tee.

"The best position to come in from is the left," advises Eastward Ho! assistant professional Paul Cannon. "It shortens the hole."

At the bottom of the fairway, there is a large bell. Ringing it alerts the group on the tee that the landing area is clear.

Your approach shot is a long iron or a fairway wood to the small green, well-protected with bunkers on both sides. Whatever you do, don't hit your approach shot to the left. You'll never find it.

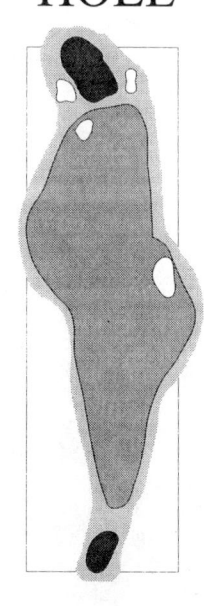

Edgartown

1927: Edgartown/627-5343

Architect: Cornelius S. Lee, Bror Hoagland
Course Rating: 68.0 **Course Slope:** 121
Course Record: 6-under 30 by Robert Chapman (9 holes)
Tee Time Policy: Private course
Amenities: Pull carts, alcohol bar, food service
The Skinny: A sporty, links-style 9-holer.
Directions: From Hyannis, Falmouth, Woods Hole, or New Bedford, you can take a ferry to Martha's Vineyard (preferably, to the Town of Oak Bluffs).

From the dock at Oak Bluffs, follow Beach Road toward Edgartown. The entrance to Edgartown is on your left, just before the triangle that marks the intersection with Vineyard Haven Road.

The Course

The oldest surviving course on the Vineyard, Edgartown Golf Club was organized when the Oak Bluffs Country Club dissolved in the 1920s. The course was the dream of Cornelius S. Lee, who purchased the Captain Chase Pease Farm, then used funds from thirty-one founding members to build the course. Before he built Edgartown, though, Lee had visited St. Andrews in Scotland, where the links course so impressed Lee that he tried his hand in the art by designing Edgartown Golf Club with the help of Bror Hoagland, the club's first superintendent. The course opened in the summer of 1927, and Lee held title of the land until 1961, when the club purchased the golf course from the Lee family. What has survived through these years is a testy 9-holer with many different looks on the second loop around the course.

Edgartown's particular uniqueness rests in the

Hol	Par	Yds	Hcp
1	4	324	9
2	5	492	1
3	4	299	13
4	5	445	5
5	4	268	15
6	3	155	17
7	4	319	7
8	3	180	11
9	4	363	3
Out	36	2,845	
10	4	336	6
11	5	480	4
12	4	286	12
13	4	372	8
14	4	288	14
15	3	112	18
16	4	309	10
17	4	285	16
18	4	379	2
In	36	2,847	
Tot	72	5,592	

fact that the course has *10* greens in play, because there are 2 greens for the 1st hole. When the 1st hole is truly the *first*, you play to the green on the left; when it becomes your 10th hole, you play to the green straight ahead, par-4.

Whether you are playing the front 9 or the back 9, also determines which of the different tees you will use on the 4th/13th, 6th/15th, and 8th/17th holes. For example, the 4th hole is a straight away, 445-yard par-5; however, as the 13th hole it is a 372-yard par-4 that doglegs to the left.

The 6th hole, though, remains a par-3. The first time around it measures 155 yards, and you hit from the same teeing area as you would for the 1st hole. The second time around, this hole is the 15th, measuring a short 112 yards from a different tee.

The 8th hole is a tough par-3. As the 17th on the back 9, however, this is a 244-yard par-4 that comes out of a chute.

8th HOLE

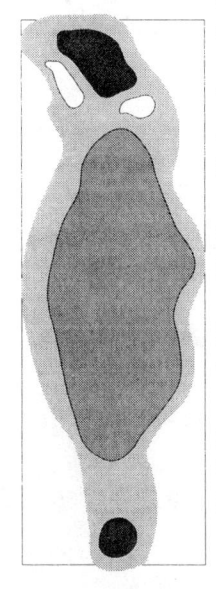

The Challenge

This is the signature hole at Edgartown Golf Club. It is a par-3 of 181 yards and is the 11th stroke hole.

It is slightly downhill. Just beyond the green is Trapps Pond. What that means is that you definitely don't want to go over the green. The water is no more than five steps beyond the putting surface.

The tee shot requires a carry over a small valley. There is a deep pot bunker in the front of the green. To the left side is a long narrow bunker.

The 8th green is one of the larger ones at Edgartown. It is 30 yards long and about 15 yards wide. There are also two levels to the green.

The prevailing wind is usually behind you, making it a cautious decision not to over club. You will hit anywhere from a 7-iron to a 3-wood on the tee, depending on the course conditions.

Falmouth

1964: E. Falmouth/548-3211

Architect: Lou Rabesa, Guy Tedesco
Course Rating: 68.8 **Course Slope:** 114
Course Record: 6-under 66 by Lynnie Bowen (1974)
Tee Time Policy: Seven days in advance
Amenities: Motor carts & pull carts, alcohol bar, food service
The Skinny: When you are golf-starved in early March, this is ready for you.

Directions: From the Bourne Bridge, take Route 28 south to Route 151. Follow Route 151 about 3½ miles east, passing both Ballymeade and the Cape Cod Country Club, until you come to Sandwich Road on your right.

Turn right onto Falmouth/Sandwich Road and travel about 2 miles. Watch for signs and turn left onto Carriage Shop Road. Falmouth will be on your right, near the intersection with Old Barnstable Road.

The Course

If you are familiar with courses in Florida, then you will be at home at Falmouth Country Club. Many holes are parallel, and the terrain, for the most part, is flat and wide open with just a few bothersome trees that line the fairways. The only water hazards you need to worry about are those where Ray's Creek meanders among the 4th to the 6th holes. Because the area is sandy-based, though, all other water drains quickly, and the course remains open for the winter whenever there is no snow on the ground . . . just like those in Florida.

The first 9 holes were built by Falmouth's original owner, Lou Rabesa with assistance from Guy Tedesco, who had been the superintendent at Wachusett Country Club and then with the Country Club of New Seabury. Among the prettiest spots on the course is their 4th hole. The shortest, this 140-yard par-3 looks like an oversized dartboard.

Hol	Par	Yds	Hcp
1	4	380	6
2	3	155	15
3	4	365	11
4	3	125	17
5	5	535	1
6	5	445	3
7	4	370	7
8	3	165	13
9	4	370	9
Out	35	2,910	
10	5	465	12
11	3	152	16
12	4	385	6
13	4	280	18
14	4	420	4
15	4	340	10
16	5	530	2
17	4	330	14
18	4	365	8
In	37	3,317	
Tot	72	6,227	

Looking down from this elevated tee, you see a green severely sloped from back-to-front. Fronting the green is the origin of Ray's Creek, a spring-fed pond with crystal clear water. To the left of the green is a huge bunker, then shrubs and scrub pines provide the backdrop for this beauty.

All things considered, Falmouth is not a serious challenge for the scratch player, but it does yield a few career rounds for the average golfer. In fact, this has been the site of the opening tournament of the Cape Cod Pro-Am League for many years.

Historically speaking, this particular course is not the *very* first one to be called Falmouth Country Club. In the 1920s, the architecture team of Wayne Stiles and John van Kleek designed an 18-hole layout in the Telegraph Hill area of Falmouth. In 1928, more than a hundred men were busily employed in the construction of the course; however, when the stock market crashed the following year, so did the original concept of a Falmouth Country Club.

5th HOLE

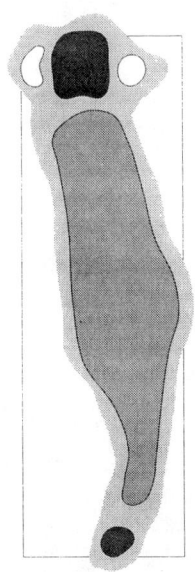

The Challenge

Few holes can jump up and bite you at Falmouth; however, this 545-yard par-5 is the No. 1 stroke hole, and it might well eat you up.

The tee shot makes it difficult, because Ray's Creek is along the right of the fairway and the left is dotted with out-of-bounds markers. Since it's a slight dogleg left, golfers who slice have trouble.

The drive, however, is not the only difficult shot. With Ray's Creek and the out-of-bounds markers squeezing the fairway, you have a smaller landing area that demands a second shot even more accurate than your first. If your ball isn't in a good lie, you'll have problems.

Most players lay up short of trouble, though, which means your third shot on the hole can be anything from the mid-iron to a fairway wood. The green is well-bunkered, both left and right, so it is difficult to avoid the sand.

Farm Neck

1976: Oak Bluffs/693-3057

Architect: Geoffrey Cornish, Peter Milligan, Brian Silva
Course Rating: 69.6 **Course Slope:** 126
Course Record: 5-under 67 by Mike Zoll and Billy Andrade
Tee Time Policy: Call two days in advance
Amenities: Motor carts & pull carts, alcohol bar, food service

The Skinny: *Every* hole is a visual adventure.
Directions: From Hyannis, Falmouth, Woods Hole, or New Bedford, you can take a ferry to Martha's Vineyard (preferably, to the Town of Oak Bluffs).

From the dock, go straight down Oak Bluffs Avenue about ¼ mile until you come to Dukes County Road on the left. Turn onto Dukes County Road and follow to the STOP sign. Turn right and continue to the Fire Station, then turn left onto County Road. Farm Neck will be along this road on the left side.

The Course

Farm Neck Golf Club had been one of New England's hidden jewels until the summer of 1993, when President Clinton decided to vacation on Martha's Vineyard and play golf. Ever since its exposure in the national media, getting a tee time here has become a difficult task.

Despite that, Farm Neck remains a wonderful course that is both scenic and strategic. It is not long, but it still provides plenty of trouble. As Mr. Clinton might now admit, this layout is similar to the Presidency: if you stray too far to the left or to the right, you will find plenty of obstacles. So, you have to be a straight-shooter to beat this course.

Geoffrey Cornish designed the front 9 at Farm Neck in 1976. Then, Peter Milligan built the back 9 a few years later. Cornish's partner, Brian Silva did much of the reconstruction.

If you last played Farm Neck before 1993, then

Hol	Par	Yds	Hcp
1	4	393	2
2	5	485	4
3	4	325	16
4	3	155	10
5	4	335	14
6	3	185	12
7	4	370	8
8	5	502	6
9	3	200	18
Out	35	2,950	
10	4	340	13
11	5	530	9
12	4	370	1
13	4	310	17
14	4	325	15
15	3	170	11
16	4	385	7
17	4	420	5
18	5	530	3
In	37	3,380	
Tot	72	6,330	

you will now find changes that make the course more playable. The 8th hole, formerly a 380-yard par-4, is now a par-5; the 280-yard 9th hole is now a 180-yard par-3; and there is now a pond, as well as a new green on the 17th.

The tee shot on the 3rd hole is an unusual mixture of beauty, opportunity, and trepidation. In the distance you see calm waters reminiscent of Bermuda. The hole is short, only 325 yards, and even a golfer of average ability is thinking *birdie*; however, in the landing area sits a gaping bunker as penal as Leavenworth.

Do not try to cut the corner on the par-5 18th hole. This is a 530-yard dogleg with out-of-bounds markers lurking all down the right. You can't get home in 2 shots, because there is a pond fronting the green. Play it cautiously. Short cuts only cause trouble.

About forty Farm Neck residents own the golf course, and the membership consists of islanders, as well as those with summer homes. Though this is open to the public, the fee for a round and a cart is probably the most expensive of any course on Cape Cod, Nantucket & Martha's Vineyard.

12th HOLE *The Challenge*

If you walk away from this hole with a par, you deserve a pat on the back. Every shot you take is fraught with danger.

A moderately-sized par-4, this measures 396 yards from the tips down to 337 yards from the front tee. You *must* think on your tee shot, for there is a huge pond that will catch long drives. Head pro Doug DeBettencourt says the best position is to the right-of-center in the fairway. Ideal tee shots from the whites are about 210 yards; from the blue tees, you can't go any farther than 235 yards.

If you pull your approach shot to the left, there is out-of-bounds, and to the right there is a bailout.

The green is protect by water in the front. It is two-tiered with several subtle breaks. You may even see some breaks that don't exist.

No doubt, this is *the* toughest hole at Farm Neck.

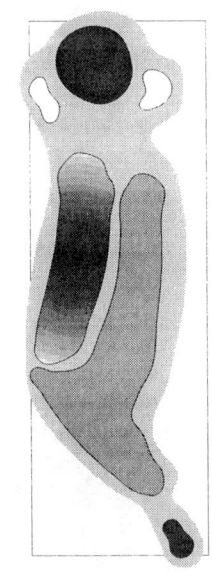

Harwichport

1918: Harwich Port/432-0250

Architect: Redesigned by Don Blakely
Course Rating: N/A **Course Slope:** N/A
Course Record: 4-under 30 by Allan Pollard
Tee Time Policy: First come, first play
Amenities: Clubhouse, rental clubs
The Skinny: Not a great course, but still a *great* place to have fun!
Directions: From the Sagamore Bridge, take Route 6 east to Exit 10. From the exit, turn right onto Route 124 south into Harwich center. With the church on your right, turn right onto Main, then immediately left onto Sisson Road, which is Route 39.

As you drive around the old Brooks Academy that is on your right, watch for Forest Street just beyond the Old Powder House along to your left. Turn left onto Forest Street, which will lead you directly to Harwichport.

The Course

Harwichport does not pretend to be anything more than it is. It will never host the US Open, the State Open, or even the Cape Cod Open.

"We don't hold *any* tournaments," says Don Blakely, who began working at the golf course as a youngster in 1952 and now operates the course. His association with this layout goes back to the days when there were a bunch of holes that actually played across the street.

Harwichport Golf Course remains just a 5-iron away from Harwich Port's center, and the increased traffic flow of today would make those holes tricky, to say the least. Playing golf would be impossible at any pace if you had to watch for passing motorists.

So Blakely redesigned the old course in the 1960s to set 4 holes on one side of the street and the remaining 5 holes on the other. As for who

Hol	Par	Yds	Hcp
1	4	358	1
2	3	170	9
3	4	340	7
4	4	330	11
5	4	325	3
6	4	255	15
7	3	155	17
8	4	295	5
9	4	310	13
Out	34	2,538	
10	4	358	2
11	3	170	10
12	4	340	8
13	4	330	12
14	4	325	4
15	4	255	16
16	3	155	18
17	4	295	6
18	4	310	14
In	34	2,538	
Tot	68	5,076	

might be responsible for that original layout, no one knows who had conceived the design. Harwichport opened in 1918.

Harwichport is a short, pedestrian, old 9-hole course. Senior citizens, beginners, and tourists who don't play much golf all can and *will* enjoy Harwichport. The fairways are flat, there are no water hazards, and only 2 holes have any bunkers.

Looking like dimes from the tee, the greens at Harwichport are not only small, but also have very little roll to them. If you can hit these greens and hold them, then you know how to play golf.

Meanwhile, Harwichport has retained something that few clubs still can claim: a ball rack. There was a time when every public club in America seemed to have a ball rack. You put your old water ball in the rack, then waited for your turn to play. You never put a new ball in the rack for fear that someone would abscond with it. Over the last ten years, though, ball racks have just about disappeared as more and more clubs go to reserved tee times.

8th HOLE

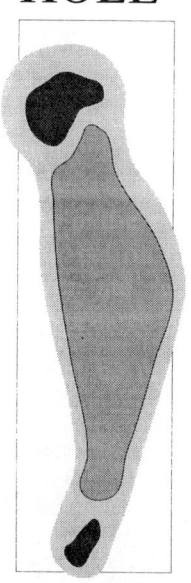

The Challenge

This hole at Harwichport is the one that Don Blakely says gives him the most trouble. A dogleg left, this is a par-4 that plays about 295 yards.

Some big hitters may try to drive the green by aiming their tee shot over the trees on the left. That straightens out the hole, but it can be very risky. Instead, Blakely advises that you try to hit your drive to put yourself in position for the second shot.

"What makes this hole so difficult is the green," notes Blakely. "It is one of our smaller ones."

Even if you hit what seems to be a good approach shot, you may wind up chipping.

Highland Links

1892: N. Truro/487-9201

Architect: Isaac and Willard Small, J.H. McKinley
Course Rating: 64.6 **Course Slope:** 100
Course Record: 8-under 62 by David Silva (1987)
Tee Time Policy: One week in advance
Amenities: Motor carts & pull carts, alcohol bar, food service
The Skinny: This is a *must* for anyone who wants to be known as a golfer.

Directions: From the Sagamore Bridge, follow Route 6 east nearly its full length until you pass Truro center. In North Truro, turn onto Highland Road. Highland Links is just past the Truro Elementary School.

The Course

Because there is nothing like Highland Links anywhere else in New England (perhaps, even in *all* of America!), this particular spot of North Truro has a special niche in the world of golf. The late Alistair Cooke, best known in America as the host of *Masterpiece Theatre*, was also an avid golfer, who once described Highland Links as the *perfect* example of the typical Scottish links: treeless and windswept, a meandering collection of 9 holes.

Though this is one of the *very* first courses on Cape Cod, Nantucket & Martha's Vineyard, the sand greens were replaced by grass greens in 1916, and Francis Ouimet came to play in the inaugural event that year. About that same time there was a terrible storm that washed three boats ashore off the adjacent Highland Light. The townsfolk hoisted one barge, the *Colerain*, up the cliffs. For many years thereafter, its pilot house served as the clubhouse.

Hol	Par	Yds	Hcp
1	4	250	11
2	5	460	7
3	3	160	13
4	5	415	5
5	4	380	1
6	5	464	3
7	3	171	15
8	4	353	9
9	3	136	17
Out	36	2,789	
10	4	242	12
11	4	377	4
12	3	118	16
13	4	346	6
14	4	361	2
15	5	453	10
16	3	159	14
17	4	349	8
18	3	105	18
In	34	2,510	
Tot	70	5,299	

If that sounds a bit more eccentric than quaint, consider the possibility that Highland Links might have had everything else. Once there had even been a net to save balls from flying off the 200-foot cliffs; however, it is gone. Gone, too, is the blind, dogleg par-3, where foursomes had to ring a bell so the next group could know when hit their tee shots. And gone are the cement greens, the miniature golf course by the 8th tee, and the bowling alley, too.

Meanwhile, Highland Links has undergone changes which some might consider more traditional. For example, what plays as the 9th hole today, had been the 1st hole. This 115-yarder received considerable attention in the 1970s when *Sports Illustrated* presented a feature on great short holes. The editors selected this as one of the best short par-3s in the *entire world*.

The layout, like many Cape Cod courses, seems to be in constant change. The last major re-routing occurred in the 1950s when Harold Conklin assumed control of the course. Conklin leased it to Antone Duarte in 1966 before the National Park Service took it over in 1967. Now the town of Truro leases it.

2nd HOLE

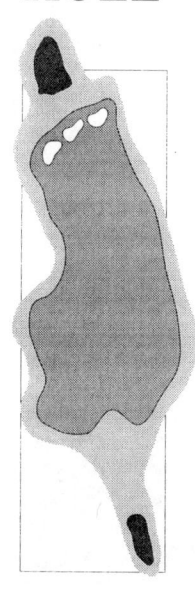

The Challenge

Being on the elevated 2nd tee transports you back into another time. Behind you stands the peninsula's oldest lighthouse; on a hill across the fairway rises a monument in memory of the 19th century Swedish nightingale, Jenny Lind. Both were seen by the first golfers playing these links.

You hit your drive on this par-5 of 480 yards into a valley surrounded by hills of hog cranberries. If you can keep this tee shot in play, you have a chance to reach the green in 2. A prevailing southwesterly wind will help you.

Though the green is guarded by 3 bunkers, they should not be used to gauge your approach. You also might think that the green is just behind the bunkers, but it is not. The putting surface is some 20 yards beyond them. Though the green is small, it is not very dangerous. Unless you are a terrible putter, you won't 3-putt.

Holly Ridge

1966: S. Sandwich/428-5577

Architect: Geoffrey Cornish
Course Rating: N/A **Course Slope:** N/A
Course Record: 6-under 48 by Fred Caouette
Tee Time Policy: One day in advance
Amenities: Motor carts & pull carts, alcohol bar, food service
The Skinny: Don't expect to eat this course up.
Directions: From the Sagamore Bridge, take Route 6 east to Exit 3. From the exit, turn right onto Quaker Meetinghouse Road south, and drive to the traffic lights that intersect with Cotuit Road. Turn left onto Cotuit Road, then take your first left onto Farmersville Road. You will come to Boardley Road on your right, which will lead you to Country Club Road and Holly Ridge.

Meanwhile, The Ridge Club is not that much further along Farmersville Road, just past Boardley Road.

The Course

Holly Ridge Golf Course may well be *the* toughest par-3 course anywhere on Cape Cod, Nantucket & Martha's Vineyard. During its first ten years of operation, not one golfer *ever* broke par! With 8 holes measuring longer than 180 yards, this layout stretches 2,952 yards overall, indeed the longest of any par-3 on the Cape & Islands.

Although tough, Holly Ridge is a beautiful par-3 created by Geoffrey Cornish, the dean of all New England golf architects. The popularity of the very first par-3 on Cape Cod, his Blue Rock layout, was the catalyst that owner Tom Niblet needed to build Holly Ridge with Daniel McCarthy.

Niblet was the head pro at The Hyannisport Club during the JFK era, and McCarthy served as the greens superintendent before Niblet gave up his position as a head professional at the prestigious private club to become a golf course owner.

Hol	Par	Yds	Hcp
1	3	163	9
2	3	183	5
3	3	142	13
4	3	158	11
5	3	120	17
6	3	184	7
7	3	187	3
8	3	130	15
9	3	202	1
Out	27	1,469	
10	3	124	16
11	3	167	10
12	3	183	7
13	3	128	18
14	3	186	8
15	3	188	4
16	3	211	2
17	3	138	14
18	3	158	16
In	27	1,469	
Tot	54	2,952	

Holly Ridge was built in conjunction with a residential community designed by architect Dean Lawrence; however, Niblet and McCarthy made certain the house lots did not converge on the golf course.

Holly Ridge was one of three par-3 courses to open on Cape Cod within a twelve-month span. Fiddler's Green (now Tara Woods) and Ashumuth Valley (Paul Harney Golf Course) started in the late 1960s. Despite soaring interest rates for real estate loans, Holly Ridge survived not only the lean years for golf courses in the early 1970s, but also the gas shortage that ate into tourism on the Cape & Islands.

Holly Ridge was the site of the old Channel 38 golf feature in the early 1970s called *The Birds-eye Classic*. In those days, Niblet would join television announcer Fred Cusick atop a station wagon with a TV camera to tape a wonderful collection of broadcasts. These served as the forerunner of the more slickly produced *Tucker Anthony Classic* that began here in the late 1980s before moving to the neighboring Ridge Club.

9th HOLE

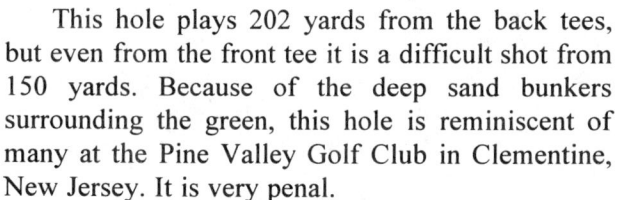

The Challenge

This hole plays 202 yards from the back tees, but even from the front tee it is a difficult shot from 150 yards. Because of the deep sand bunkers surrounding the green, this hole is reminiscent of many at the Pine Valley Golf Club in Clementine, New Jersey. It is very penal.

The green is subtly sloped from back-to-front; however, you'd better hit the green on-the-fly, because you can't run it on. There just isn't a big enough opening. One huge bunker goes from the middle front around the right side of the green to the back. There are 2 bunkers on the left side.

If your tee shot is so far off line that it misses the green *and* the bunkers, you are in trouble. Your ball will bounce into the scrub pines and oaks that line the hole.

A 3 on the 9th usually wins the hole.

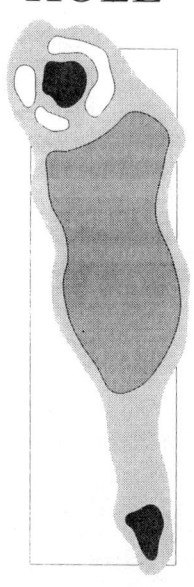

Hyannis

1973: Hyannis/362-2606

Architect: Geoffrey Cornish, William G. Robinson
Course Rating: 69.0 **Course Slope:** 118
Course Record: 5-under 66 by Jack Sances
Tee Time Policy: One month in advance if prepaid
Amenities: Motor carts & pull carts, alcohol bar, food service
The Skinny: Great place for a winter game of golf. Well-protected from the elements.

Directions: From the Sagamore Bridge, take Route 6 east to Exit 6. From the exit, turn right onto Route 132 south and watch for the course just short of a mile along on your left.

Because Route 132 can have some unforgiving traffic, you might want to prepare for the entrance to Hyannis. A telling sign will be the power lines that cross above Route 132 not far before the course.

The Course

When Wollaston golfer Fordie Pitts and his group of limited partners purchased this course in 1989, they made changes. All of them were for the better. One obvious change was that they renamed the course from Iyanough Hills Golf Club to Hyannis Golf Club.

Beyond that, though, they switched the 9s. What had been the 1st hole, a straightaway par-5, became the 10th. Even then, those were only superficial changes.

Another change was the sort that all golfers could appreciate: the condition of the greens. Dave Porkka, the director of golf, credits greens superintendent Russ Bragdon with doing a terrific job in bringing these greens around. "Some," says Porkka, "have called them the best public greens on the Cape." And well they might be.

Though the remaining changes might seem

Hol	Par	Yds	Hcp
1	4	362	13
2	4	420	1
3	4	340	9
4	4	400	3
5	5	528	5
6	4	345	15
7	3	114	17
8	3	195	11
9	4	406	7
Out	35	3,110	
10	4	490	8
11	4	225	16
12	4	380	4
13	4	325	12
14	5	515	6
15	3	148	18
16	4	310	14
17	4	345	10
18	4	400	2
In	36	3,290	
Tot	72	6,400	

insignificant, they are among the very things that golfers are happy to see. There are no new holes, or even new greens. The bunkers are still the same. Instead, Hyannis Golf Club upgraded the driving range and cleaned out a lot of the woods so you can easily find your ball if it is in there.

Overall, this course should be noted as a haven for winter golfers. Players from as far away as Boston and Providence travel to Hyannis Golf Club on weekend mornings for their golfing fix. When the Cape Cod Pro-Am League shuts down in mid-December, there is an informal winter pro-am every Wednesday at Hyannis. Weather permitting, it continues until the Cape Cod Pro-Am League opens up again in March.

The Cape Cod Pro-Am League comes to Hyannis Golf Course once a year, and the final round of the Cape Cod Open is co-hosted by Hyannis and Olde Barnstable Fairgrounds. Twice Hyannis has been the second-round host of the prestigious Southeast Amateur.

2nd HOLE

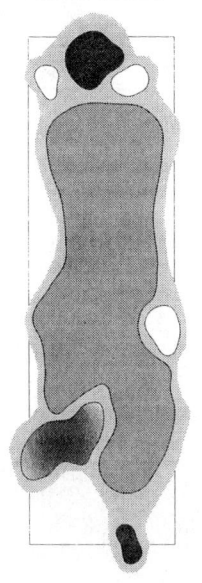

The Challenge

Much longer than its posted 420 yards, this hole can be a beast. It plays directly into the prevailing wind, which is why it ranks as the toughest hole on the golf course.

"You stand on the tee, and you see water," notes Dave Porkka. "Then, you have to hit a good tee shot to get over it."

That water is slightly to the left, and there is a fairway bunker at the corner of the dogleg.

Reaching the green with your second shot is a tough assignment. An uphill shot to an elevated green protected by 2 bunkers, there is a small area to run the ball up to the green, which has two levels.

"If you are thinking of 1-putting it," advises Porkka, "you need to be on the right tier."

If the pin is near the middle on the left hand side, you are in trouble.

Hyannisport

1908: Hyannisport/775-2978

Architect: Alex Finlay, (r) Donald Ross, Frederick Paine, Ron Forse
Course Rating: 70.4 **Course Slope:** 128
Course Record: 8-under 63 by Mark Chasson (1989)
Tee Time Policy: Private course
Amenities: Motor carts, alcohol bar, food service
The Skinny: If the wind's blowing, it's a new game.
Directions: From the Sagamore Bridge, take Route 6 east to Exit 6. From the exit, turn right onto Route 132 south and prepare for the turn. After the first set of traffic lights, bear right at the Cape Codder Hotel onto Bearse's Way. This follows for a mile, crosses Route 28 at a traffic light, then continues another mile to a light at North Street.

At North Street, turn right and follow to the West End Rotary, where the traffic circulates past West Main, Scudder Avenue, Main Street and North Street again in that order. From the rotary, take Scudder Avenue.

Follow Scudder about a mile, but travel straight when it begins to bear right and becomes Craigville Beach Road. Follow Scudder Avenue to Irving Avenue, then turn right. The entrance to Hyannisport sits just beyond St. Andrew's.

The Course

Hyannisport is truly one of the great courses in New England. Along with its links-style layout, its dime-size greens are legendary, always remaining a challenge to hit as the constant southwesterly winds blow throughout the summer.

Formerly the Marchant Farm, Hyannisport was a site for playing golf after the turn of the century. The club was born in 1908 when Alex Finlay designed the first layout. Later, Hyannisport hired Donald Ross to design the course; however, construction costs seemed lavish for Hyannisport's members. So Ross departed, but he left his plans, which were used by a member, Frederick Paine, to expand the layout to an 18-hole course.

There have been a few changes made to Hyannisport. The 3rd hole is a wonderful dogleg left over a marsh, and the club has extended the marsh so that the green looks like an island.

Hol	Par	Yds	Hcp
1	4	448	3
2	4	265	17
3	4	353	7
4	4	410	1
5	3	177	15
6	5	514	11
7	4	388	9
8	3	194	13
9	5	505	5
Out	36	3,254	
10	4	392	4
11	4	420	2
12	4	391	6
13	4	308	16
14	4	374	8
15	3	178	12
16	4	480	10
17	3	143	18
18	4	310	14
In	35	2,996	
Tot	71	6,260	

In addition, the University of Rhode Island Turf School in Kingstown, Rhode Island, grew a new 4th green during the 1993 season.

Still, it is the wind that makes Hyannisport so interesting.

The 17th hole is an extraordinary 147-yard par-3, and this proved to be the case in 1989, when the Massachusetts Golf Association held the State Four-Ball Championship at Hyannisport. On the first day, the wind was at the players' backs, and the eventual champion Jon Fasick hit a wedge to the green. The second day, though, the wind was in their faces, and those same players were hitting 2-irons into the wind.

The highlight of the season is its kickoff tournament, The Seagulls, held every April. Those who have experienced the weeks that are known as "spring" on the Cape & Islands will understand that the weather conditions for this tournament are nothing less than arduous. In addition, Hyannisport is the site of the Cape Cod Amateur, which wraps up the season every November.

4th HOLE

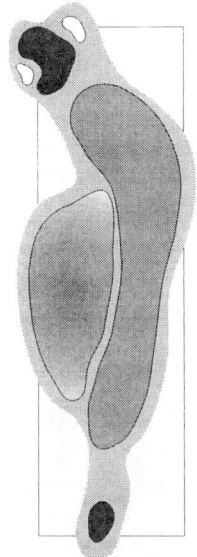

The Challenge

This 410-yard par-4 hole is a wonderful bite-off hole. You stand on the tee and see the fairway curve to the left around the marsh. Then you try to judge how much of the dogleg you can carry.

"Try to play it as close to the marsh as you dare," says Chris Davies, Hyannisport's assistant professional. The bailout area is to the right; however, if you hit it too far right, you will have a fairway wood to a sloped green. That is, *if* you can reach the green.

Usually, the wind is behind you on the tee. On your approach shot, however, the prevailing wind is from left to right. Davies says that means you have to start your shot over the marsh and let the wind bring your ball in.

That makes it even more difficult to hit the green.

Kings Way

1988: Yarmouthport/362-8820

Architect: Brian Silva
Course Rating: 58.9 **Course Slope:** 93
Course Record: 3-under 56 by Tom Cavicchi
Tee Time Policy: Three days in advance
Amenities: Motor carts, alcohol bar, food service
The Skinny: Play this soon, before it becomes a private course.
Directions: From the Sagamore Bridge, take Route 6 east to Exit 8. From the ramp, turn left and cross beneath Route 6. (This is Union Street; however, if you turn right from the exit, this road is called Station Avenue). Follow Union Street north to the flashing yellow light at the intersection with Route 6A, then turn right. The entrance to Kings Way is about 2 miles east on Route 6A on your left.

The Course

If you want to play Kings Way Golf Club, you should play it soon. After the final condominiums are sold, this residential community course will become a private facility. Meanwhile, the course already has that private course ambience. You are given the royal treatment normally accorded private course golfers, and the conditions are as good as you will find at any private course on Cape Cod, Nantucket & Martha's Vineyard. The bentgrass fairways, tees, and greens have grown in nicely since the course opened in 1988.

For this executive course (par 59/4,100 yards), perception is the only problem.

"A lot of golfers are snobs," says Ed Bullock, who publishes the *Cape Cod Golf Guide* and operates the food service at Kings Way. "They think an executive course is inferior; however, once they get past that, Kings Way surprises them. The

Hol	Par	Yds	Hcp
1	4	346	5
2	3	198	7
3	3	155	11
4	4	375	1
5	3	124	17
6	3	189	9
7	3	157	13
8	3	147	15
9	4	409	3
Out	30	2,100	
10	3	215	14
11	3	193	12
12	4	297	4
13	3	167	18
14	3	167	8
15	3	138	10
16	3	181	16
17	3	211	6
18	4	354	2
In	29	1,923	
Tot	59	4,023	

holes at our course could fit into any of the top courses on the Cape."

Designed by Brian Silva, Kings Way has treacherous, yet beautiful par-3s mixed with strategic par-4s. The 375-yard 4th hole, for example, is a par-4 that requires a long carry over a waste area. The 9th hole, a 409-yard par-4, demands either a long iron, or a fairway wood to a small green. It belongs on any championship course.

Though the distances from the greens to the next tees are close on the front 9, they are longer on the back 9 because of condominiums.

Still, that doesn't make these holes any less inviting.

The 10th is a long, uphill par-3 of 215 yards; you'd better not miss the 12th hole to the right because of the water hazard; and the finishing holes are just as treacherous. The 17th is another uphill par-3 to a two-tiered green that rarely sees a par, and the 18th is a slight dogleg left, par-4 with bunkers straddling the right side of the fairway.

14th HOLE *The Challenge*

This is the signature hole at Kings Way. From the back tee, a saltmarsh provides a spectacular backdrop, and on a clear day you can see Cape Cod Bay.

It plays 167 yards from the back tees and 104 yards from the front. Because of the nearby bay, the wind often comes into play in your club selection. Though you can hit anything, assistant professional Mark Surette says, "It's usually a 6-iron, but it can be as much as a 4-iron."

You play from an elevated tee to a rolling green below, where a cloverleaf sand bunker protects the front left of the deceptive green.

"Most greens are high back-to-front, but this one is higher in the front," notes Surette. That contour gives you the illusion that the green is flat. If your ball is on the front of the green, and the pin is in the back, however, it is a downhill putt.

Kittansett

1923: Marion/748-0192

Architect: Frederic C. Hood, William S. Flynn (r)
Course Rating: 72.2 **Course Slope:** 131
Course Record: 4-under 67 by Robert Parente (1978)
Tee Time Policy: Private course that must be played with a club member or staff member.
Amenities: Motor carts & pull carts, caddies, alcohol bar, food service
The Skinny: If you get a chance to play this course, don't pass it up!

Directions: From the Sagamore Bridge, follow Route 6 west through Wareham center. Beyond Wareham center, take a left onto Marion Road, which is still Route 6. About 5 miles down the road, take a left at the traffic lights onto Point Road.
 This will wind for another 4 miles, passing Little Marion, until it ends at the Kittansett Club.

The Course

Local golfers from the Cape & Islands had known that this was a great track long before it was "discovered" by the rest of the world in 1953. That was when the famed Walker Cup competition was hosted by Kittansett, whose name is the Native American word meaning *near the sea*.

"I fell in love at first sight," exclaimed British writer Leonard Cawley of this links-style course. "How strange that one never sees an old-fashioned bunker [in America] as we have at St. Andrew's. They are there at Kittansett, however, and to the British player, it feels like home."

Noted architect Robert Trent Jones called it "one of the short courses capable of holding a national championship," and golf experts continue to rank this among the Top 100 courses in America.

The architect of Kittansett was a club member, Frederic C. Hood, and this was the only course he

Hol	Par	Yds	Hcp
1	4	430	5
2	4	425	11
3	3	165	17
4	4	360	7
5	4	410	1
6	4	390	13
7	5	530	3
8	3	205	15
9	4	390	9
Out	35	3,305	
10	4	345	16
11	3	240	12
12	4	395	2
13	4	365	8
14	3	180	18
15	5	525	6
16	4	400	10
17	4	395	4
18	5	490	14
In	36	3,335	
Tot	71	6,640	

ever built. In the process, more than 100,000 tons of rocks were unearthed from this craggy shoreline at the end of Butler's Point, and workmen carved fairways from its heavily-wooded areas. While the felled trees and uprooted stumps were easily disposed of in bonfires, the stones and boulders that had been deposited here by glaciers presented a much greater problem. Piled at strategic locations, then covered with dirt and loam, though, they became man-made mounds that give this otherwise flat, coastal plain its rather unusual definition.

Meanwhile, other features of Kittansett further lend an air of uniqueness. Hood, for example, cleverly arranged all but 2 holes so that you rarely play from the tee directly into the sun. And on those 2 holes where the sun might be a factor, it can happen only during a few times of the day and *never* in the same round.

Hood also designed every hole so that you can see the base of the pin from the vantage of the appropriate approach shot. And except for the sand that encircles the 3rd hole, none of Kittansett's 59 bunkers is located behind any of its greens.

17th HOLE *The Challenge*

Though not as dramatic as the island-green 3rd hole, this one is just as deadly. The straightaway par-4 plays at 395 yards from the back tees down to 315 from the red markers. It is the only blind tee shot, so you can't see a brook crossing the fairway.

Usually, the wind comes whipping off Marion Harbor, where it sweeps across Point Road, over the green, up the fairway, and right into your face as you stand on the tee.

"If the wind is at your back," says long-time head professional Tom Shea, "the long hitter has to lay up with an iron."

Behind the green is a house, to the right of which is a telephone pole that is a good target for your tee shot. To the right of the green is a bunker, and another protects the front left. The green has a gentle slope, but the speed of the green will make it severe.

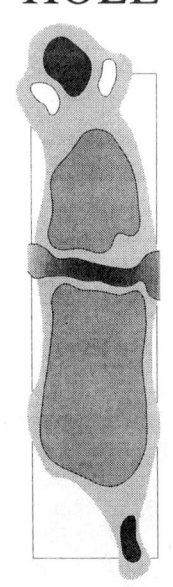

Little Harbor

1963: Wareham/295-2617

Architect: Richard Bowler, Sam Mitchell
Course Rating: N/A **Course Slope:** N/A
Course Record: 7-under 49 by Mike Mann (par 56); 6-under 49 by Robert Hunter (par 55)
Tee Time Policy: Three days in advance
Amenities: Motor carts & pull carts, alcohol bar, food service
The Skinny: An off-the-beaten-track, fun spot.

Directions: From the Sagamore Bridge, take Route 6 west into Wareham. Just beyond the fork where Route 6 splits to become one-way east, turn left at the traffic light onto Depot Street. At the next set of lights, Depot Street crosses the other fork of Route 6 that heads west. Stay on Depot Street, which becomes Great Neck Road. Follow this winding road about 4½ miles to Little Harbor.

The Course

Unlike some other courses, where the mood is cut-throat and where everybody wants to get into a Nassau on the 1st tee, the atmosphere at Little Harbor Golf Course seems more like one big family.

Located on the coastal plain near Wareham's Little Harbor (hence, its name), Little Harbor Golf Course is fairly flat. Of the 18 holes here, 13 are tree-lined, and there are 2 water holes. The average size of a green is about 5,200 square feet.

This executive course was once a farm owned by Richard Bowler, who built the course with the help of architect Samuel Mitchell. When it opened in June of 1963, Little Harbor was a par-3; however, 2 holes were expanded to par-4s, thus making it a par 56. Later, the owners added 2 bunkers, then planted more than 50 trees to beautify the golf course.

Hol	Par	Yds	Hcp
1	3	100	17
2	3	135	15
3	3	142	13
4	3	138	7
5	3	225	1
6	4	291	5
7	4	275	9
8	3	162	11
9	3	189	3
Out	29	1,657	
10	3	205	4
11	3	125	10
12	3	140	14
13	3	132	12
14	3	183	6
15	3	100	18
16	3	156	8
17	3	132	16
18	3	208	2
In	27	1,381	
Tot	56	3,038	

on Cape Cod, Nantucket & Martha's Vineyard

As with all courses that have a majority of par-3 holes, there are plenty of aces. Take, for example, the feat of Louis Uva, a club member whose 1-shotters made the pages of *Sports Illustrated*. On one particular Saturday in the 1980s, Uva knocked a 7-iron into the cup on the 135-yard 2nd hole, and he thought it was a big deal.

The next day, he stood on the tee with his 7-iron and told the others it would *never* again happen in a million years. Louis Uva, however, proved himself wrong and aced the 2nd hole one more time!

As if that weren't amazing enough, club member Carl Bump had *two* holes-in-one during a single round in the early 1990s!

You have ample opportunity to create some excitement of your own, for Little Harbor is one of those courses that remains open year round, weather permitting.

18th HOLE — *The Challenge*

The finishing hole at any course should be a test when a match is in the balance, or a course record is on the line. This is just that type of hole.

The fairway is tree-lined, and the green is 208 yards from the members' tees with a water hazard to the left. The wind here is key. Behind the green flies an American flag above a memorial stone to the course's builder, Richard Bowler. You should check that flag to see which way the wind blows. It's usually in your face. Otherwise, it might be blowing across, drawing your ball into the hazard.

The large green is fairly flat, and there are no bunkers; however, it is framed by 3 subtle mounds that kick off shots and guard pin placements.

Member Michael Mann will never forget the test this hole provides. He needed a par to be the first golfer ever to shoot an 8-under 48; however, he bogeyed the hole, tying the mark for low round.

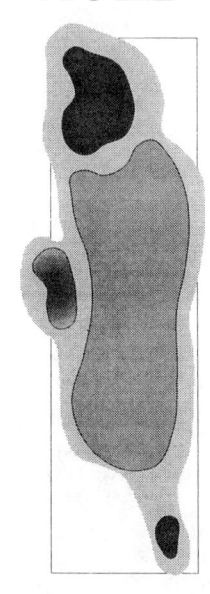

Little Marion

1906: Marion/748-0199

Architect: George C. Thomas
Course Rating: 67.0 **Course Slope:** 116
Course Record: Unknown
Tee Time Policy: None
Amenities: Pull carts, clubhouse, snack bar
The Skinny: You should play it without keeping track of your score.
Directions: From the Sagamore Bridge, follow Route 6 west through Wareham center. Beyond Wareham center, take a left onto Marion Road, which is still Route 6. About 5 miles down the road, take a left at the traffic lights onto Point Road. This will wind for about 1 mile, and you will find Little Marion on your right.

The Course

While Highland Links in North Truro might be the closest you can come to playing a *Scottish* links course this side of the Atlantic, Little Marion might well be your closest to a true *English* course.

"Either you love the course, or you hate it," says Sue Rezendes, who operates this course with her husband, Joe. There is no in-between. The tees are small, fairways uneven (preferred lies in your own fairway), and the greens are the sizes of dimes.

Look at the 1st hole and you will see a berm straddling the fairway. When they built the course, they took the rocks and waste material and covered them over to make berms such as that. Added to them throughout are criss-crossing stonewalls that appear more like a steeplechase course than a golf course. There is one juncture of stonewalls behind the 9th tee and another in front of the 8th green. And if all that were not enough, the rough is high

Hol	Par	Yds	Hcp
1	4	315	15
2	4	290	11
3	3	175	7
4	5	460	13
5	4	365	9
6	4	430	1
7	4	365	5
8	3	180	3
9	3	115	17
Out	34	2,695	
10	4	315	16
11	4	290	12
12	3	175	8
13	5	460	14
14	4	365	10
15	4	430	2
16	4	365	6
17	3	180	4
18	3	115	18
In	34	2,695	
Tot	68	5,390	

and ample, and grass hummocks abound to divert your errant shots into even more trouble.

Around the turn of the century, Little Marion began as a makeshift, par 9 3-hole course on the Bulliard farm. George C. Thomas remodeled those first 3 holes and added 6 more. This was his first project before he worked with Donald Ross and A.W. Tillinghast on other projects; he also worked with Hugh Wilson at Merion GC in Pennsylvania, as well as George Crump at Pine Valley in New Jersey. The Bulliards eventually sold the course to a land trust that leases it out; however, the Rezendes family does not advertise their little gem, because golfers who get caught up in scores usually don't enjoy Little Marion.

Still, when you enter the clubhouse, which is a converted farm house built in 1825, you realize that this *is* different. Displayed along the walls in primitive surroundings are yellowed photographs of former club champions, as well as a tarnished trophy that has passed from club champion to club champion for more than 80 years.

9th HOLE

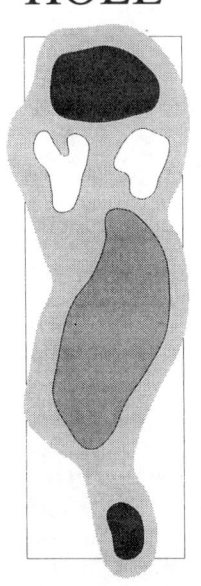

The Challenge

The first hole you see when you park your car and walk to the clubhouse is this: the shortest. The first thing that strikes you about it are mammoth bunkers rising like sentinels guarding the green. These are unlike anything else you will see anywhere on Cape Cod, Nantucket & Martha's Vineyard, if not anywhere in *all* of New England.

Though these are unnaturally high, a stone wall between the green and the bunker braces it. This wall is one of many on the course from glacial boulders dug up when they cut the farmland, then the course out of this thickly-wooded area. You can see a few boulders near the top of the bunker.

The hole measures a treacherous 115 yards. All that you see from the tee is the flag's top in the breeze. If you are talented enough to put your tee shot on the green, there is still work ahead for you. The putting surface is a treacherous, sloping green.

Miacomet

1964: Nantucket/228-9764

Architect: Ralph Marble
Course Rating: 71.2 **Course Slope:** 113
Course Record: 5-under 69 by Bill Medeiros and Peter Benson
Tee Time Policy: One week
Amenities: Motor carts & pull carts, alcohol bar, food service
The Skinny: You'd better have a punch shot to play this course.

Directions: From Hyannis or Woods Hole, you can take a ferry to Nantucket. Follow the head of Main Street out of town and turn left to follow New Mill about ¼ of a mile. At Prospect Street, turn left and follow South Prospect about ½ mile to Surfside Road. Turn right onto Surfside for another ¼ mile before you turn right onto Bartlett Road. Follow Bartlett its full length of 1 mile or so, and this will end at West Miacomet Road and Miacomet.

The Course

When Nantucket farmer Ralph Marble built this 9-hole course in 1964, it was not the first recreation facility he had built on this property. Already, Marble had tennis courts and pony rides, as well as a small go-cart track.

These days, though, the Nantucket farmer no longer owns any of it. Instead, this belongs to the Nantucket Land Bank Council, which is licensed by the Commonwealth of Massachusetts to purchase land for recreational and conservation purposes. Miacomet has remained a golf course in order to provide the island with preserved open space, and this links-style course is nothing if it is not *open space*.

"When the wind blows, there is nothing to stop it," says Charlie Stackpole, who has operated the golf course since 1988. "Sometimes you need an extra club or two. Sometimes you have to hit three

Hol	Par	Yds	Hcp
1	4	374	9
2	4	332	15
3	4	384	13
4	4	367	3
5	3	163	17
6	4	407	5
7	5	463	11
8	4	378	1
9	5	469	7
Out	37	3,337	
10	4	375	10
11	4	332	16
12	4	384	14
13	4	367	4
14	3	163	18
15	4	407	6
16	5	463	12
17	4	378	2
18	5	469	8
In	37	3,337	
Tot	74	6,674	

or four extra clubs, depending on how strong the wind is blowing."

Flat and easy to walk, Miacomet is not a manicured course; however, it isn't too funky, either. Yet, if you miss the narrow fairways, you are in trouble. The rough can be laborious.

"It's not that the rough is long," Stackpole explains. "It's just that [your ball] can bury easily."

None of which frightens away any golfers. Miacomet was a sleepy golf course once upon a time, but the number of rounds being played continues to increase each year, and the course is fast becoming busy. In 1993, for example, more than 27,000 rounds were played at Miacomet. That's up more than 35% from the previous years, and it will become even busier.

Ohio architect Michael Hurdzan, the designer who built The Willowbend Club and The Dennis Highlands, has drawn plans to expand this island course into a championship layout. Pending approval from the Commonwealth and all the permitting boards, Miacomet will have the island's second championship golf course.

4th HOLE

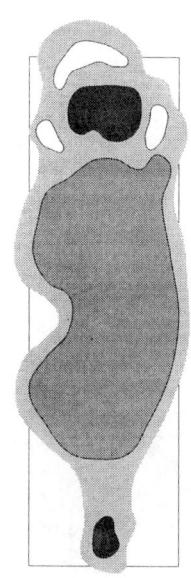

The Challenge

Look at the scorecard when you get to this hole, and you will notice that this isn't the longest par-4 on the course. It's only 364 yards, and there are 4 other par-4s that are longer. You'll see that the 4th hole isn't the lowest handicap hole, either. That honor goes to the 378-yard 8th hole.

"However, this is the most challenging hole as far as I'm concerned," says head professional Charlie Stackpole. "You don't get much roll to your drive because of the uphill grade of the fairway, and the prevailing wind is usually in your face."

Two gaping bunkers protect the green, but there is a 10-yard gap that will allow you to run the ball on. A third lingers in the rear. The green is severely sloped from back-to-front, so just hope that the pin isn't near the crown.

Mink Meadows

1936: Vineyard Haven/693-0600

Architect: N/A
Course Rating: 68.6 **Course Slope:** 117
Course Record: 3-under 67 by Lynn Vanderhoop, Steve Garvin (competitive); 5-under 65 by Edd Barmakian
Tee Time Policy: One day in advance
Amenities: Motor carts & pull carts
The Skinny: Either play early, or else play late, because those are the hours when it's prettiest.
Directions: From Hyannis, Falmouth, Woods Hole, or New Bedford, you can take a ferry to Martha's Vineyard (preferably, to Vineyard Haven).

From the dock at Vineyard Haven, take your left onto Water Street and follow to the first stop sign. Turn right onto Beach Road, go uphill, then take your first right onto Main Street. Along Main, your third left is Church Street, where you will turn and follow to Franklin Street. Turn right onto Franklin. Mink Meadows is about 2 miles up the road.

The Course

Before it was established as a golf course in 1936, this was a mink farm; hence, its name: Mink Meadows, one of the older courses on Martha's Vineyard.

This links course nearly disappeared a few years ago until a group of golfers banded together to purchase and preserve Mink Meadows, which has always has been 9 holes. Robert Bigelow built the golf course; however, no one knows whether or not a professional architect did any of the design work. The Mink Meadows Association operates the golf course these days, and though trees had been cut for another 9 holes, the back 9 was never built.

Meanwhile, thanks to superintendent Tom Wessner, the condition of this course dramatically changed in the early 1990s. The former All-America golfer at Springfield College improved the turf condition with a watering system that enables

Hol	Par	Yds	Hcp
1	4	339	11
2	4	314	13
3	4	354	5
4	4	410	1
5	3	165	15
6	4	401	3
7	3	156	17
8	5	497	9
9	4	373	7
Out	35	3,002	
10	4	339	12
11	4	314	14
12	4	354	6
13	4	410	2
14	3	165	16
15	4	401	4
16	3	156	18
17	5	497	10
18	4	373	8
In	35	3,002	
Tot	70	6,004	

the course to stay green throughout the summer and prevents your tee shots from running like they used to. Before they put in the automated watering system, hired workers went out at 4 every afternoon and hand-watered the 9 holes until midnight.

Mink Meadows may be one of the smallest courses on the Cape & Islands; however, what it lacks in size it makes up for with panoramic views of the Atlantic Ocean. And while this might not be the most prestigious golf course on the islands, it is certainly one of the busiest. Golfers tee it up from sunrise to sunset at Mink Meadows.

Among them in 1993 was President Clinton. On the 455-yard par-4 4th hole, he hit a driver and a pitching wedge to the green during his first loop. On his second time around, he hit a driver from the back tee, then a 7-iron. His score: 13-over 83.

4th HOLE

The Challenge

If you can par this hole, then you're good enough to play *any* course on Cape Cod, Nantucket & Martha's Vineyard. This is a tough, uphill hole.

Measuring 455 yards from the back tees, the 4th is a slight dogleg to the right, and your second shot is to an elevated green.

"And when you play it in the summer," says head professional Tim Spring, "the wind is usually in your face."

On the tee, Spring says, you should aim to the left of the tree in the middle of the fairway. If you hit a good drive, you will still have a long iron or a fairway wood for a second shot. If you are in between clubs, you should take a little more.

There are 2 greenside bunkers that can be nasty, and the green itself is slippery.

"You don't want a downhill putt here," warns Spring.

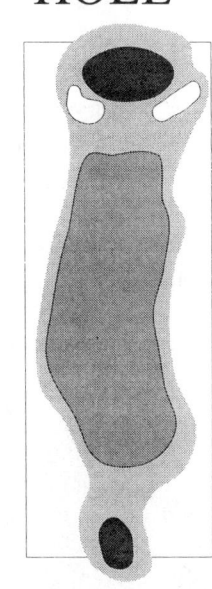

New Seabury

1964: Mashpee/477-9400

Architect: William Mitchell, (r) Rees Jones
Blue Course Rating: 73.8 **Blue Course Slope:** 138
Green Course Rating: 67.7 **Green Course Slope:** 110
Blue Course Record: 8-under 64 by Bill Ezinicki
Green Course Record: 9-under 61 by Andy Morse
Tee Time Policy: Open to public Labor Day to Memorial Day. One day advance.
Amenities: Motor & pull carts, alcohol bar, food service
The Skinny: Best course on the Cape & Islands open to the Common Man (that is, from Labor Day until Memorial Day).
Directions: From the Bourne Bridge, take Route 28 south to Route 151. Follow Route 151 east *all the way* to its end at the Mashpee/New Seabury Rotary.

As you enter the rotary, plan to *pass* the first right (Route 28), then take the second. Follow the signs that lead to New Seabury about 4½ miles further south.

The Course

Since the day that the Country Club of New Seabury opened in 1964, national trade publications have ranked it among the top resort courses.

The Blue Course is of championship caliber, and the late Francis Ouimet called it "the Pebble Beach of the East." Its first 9 holes stretch out along Nantucket Sound, making it one of *the* most picturesque courses. No doubt, the 3rd hole is the most-photographed golf hole in New England.

What makes the Blue's front 9 so challenging, though, is the wind. When it was clocked at than 30 miles an hour at the '93 State Mid-Amateur, the game was virtually impossible to play. Putts kept rolling off the green, and *no one* broke 80 the first day of the tournament.

The back 9 is wooded, but just as treacherous as the front 9 with tricky putting surfaces on every green.

BLUE COURSE

Hol	Par	Yds	Hcp
1	5	530	9
2	4	415	7
3	4	425	1
4	3	230	15
5	5	500	5
6	4	400	11
7	4	435	13
8	3	230	17
9	4	440	3
Out	36	3,605	
10	5	530	8
11	3	210	18
12	4	410	14
13	4	415	4
14	3	220	16
15	5	540	2
16	4	400	6
17	4	430	10
18	4	440	12
In	36	3,595	
Tot	72	7,200	

on Cape Cod, Nantucket & Martha's Vineyard

Meanwhile, the Green Course remains the unsung sister at New Seabury. Though it is not as long as the Blue, it definitely requires more accuracy off the tee.

New England architect William Mitchell designed both the Blue and the Green Courses. Then Rees Jones, who had reconstructed The Country Club in Brookline, Massachusetts before the 1988 US Open, remodeled some of the holes on both of New Seabury's courses.

While these courses are not open to the public from Memorial Day through Labor Day, the public is welcome to play at New Seabury after that.

Hol	Par	Yds	Hcp
1	4	431	1
2	3	218	15
3	4	288	13
4	4	340	5
5	4	306	6
6	4	310	11
7	4	337	7
8	3	192	17
9	5	483	3
Out	35	2,905	
10	4	432	4
11	3	191	18
12	5	525	6
13	4	327	12
14	4	327	10
15	5	470	2
16	3	190	16
17	3	188	14
18	4	384	8
In	35	3,034	
Tot	70	5,939	

3rd HOLE

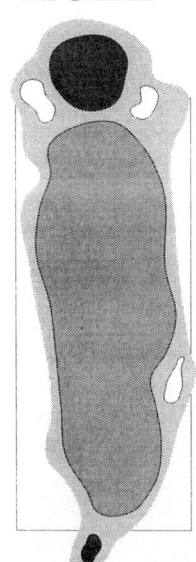

The Challenge

Whenever you see an advertisement for New Seabury's nationally-ranked Blue Course, more often than not you will see a picture of this hole. But picture this, too: it is the furthest hole away from the clubhouse and into Nantucket Sound.

A straightaway par-4, measuring 425 yards from the back and 361 yards from the front, this has always been the No. 1 stroke hole. But it got a *lot* tougher after Hurricane Bob in August of 1991.

"We used to play the beach along the right side as a hazard," notes head pro Mike Pry. "For the last two years it is out-of-bounds." That makes it a lot tougher. If you pull your drive, you have to re-tee. Pry usually uses a 3-wood or a 2-iron, and if he lands in the fairway bunker, he'll take it. "If I wind up in the fairway," he says, "all the better."

Sloped from back-to-front, this windswept green remains treacherous and subject to 3-putts.

Ocean Edge

1986: Brewster/896-5911

Architect: Brian Silva, Geoffrey Cornish
Course Rating: 71.9 **Course Slope:** 129
Course Record: 6-under 66 by Steve Whillock (1988)
Tee Time Policy: One day in advance (longer, if prepaid)
Amenities: Motor carts & pull carts, alcohol bar, food service
The Skinny: Don't let the bad shots get to you, and you will play better.
Directions: From the Sagamore Bridge, take Route 6 east to Exit 11. From the exit ramp, turn right on Route 137. Follow for 2½ miles. Ocean Edge is on the right.

The Course

Architects Brian Silva and Geoffrey Cornish were coming off their success with the neighboring Captains Course when Ocean Edge also came into existence with a great deal of fanfare in 1986.

Though they're both in the Town of Brewster, the difference between The Captains and Ocean Edge is extreme. The Captains was a typical Cape Cod, town-owned course of open fairways cut through thick woodlands; however, Ocean Edge was more of a penal golf course. Silva and Cornish threaded the 18 holes of Ocean Edge through condominiums and wetlands on grounds that once had been the Brewster Greens Golf Course.

For seven years, the New England Professional Golfers' Association (NE PGA) held its annual championship here. At first, players complained about its difficulty, and they criticized the course, because it took the driver out of their hands.

Hol	Par	Yds	Hcp
1	4	306	11
2	4	425	3
3	4	340	17
4	4	401	5
5	4	356	9
6	4	337	13
7	3	181	15
8	5	601	1
9	4	360	7
Out	36	3,307	
10	4	316	16
11	4	358	12
12	3	160	18
13	5	571	6
14	4	391	8
15	4	320	14
16	4	429	4
17	3	216	10
18	5	597	2
In	36	3,358	
Tot	72	6,665	

Because of its 6,600 yards, in fact, the average golfer must hit a driver and must hit it *straight*, due to assorted bunkers, including several Scottish-styled *pot* bunkers.

Another factor that bothered the pros, though, was the par-5s. Professionals see par-5s as make-up holes, the best opportunities for birdies. At Ocean Edge, however, 3 par-5s are Herculean: 601 yards, 571 yards and 597 yards. They aren't birdied easily.

Over the years, director of golf Ron Hallett has heeded most suggestions from the pros who have played in the championship.

Cleaning the right side of the 11th fairway, workers removed a tree blocking any approach shot. Then they filled in a nasty fairway sand bunker on the monstrous dogleg 13th hole. And on the 18th, some trees were cut down along the right side of the fairway.

Nowadays, the NE PGA players have changed their opinions about Ocean Edge and have even found out how to solve its mysteries, as attested by Steve Whillock of The Country Club, who fashioned a 6-under 66.

8th HOLE

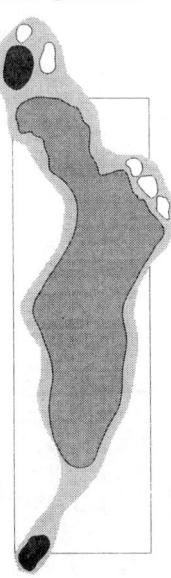

The Challenge

Though not very old, this 601-yard hole is an "Untouchable." From the back tees, you must hit your drive at least 225 yards out of a chute. No one has *ever* reached this par-5 in 2 blows, and it probably will remain forever so. At 546 yards from the middle tees, this requires a Herculean effort for the average golfer. You must hit your second shot onto a shelf, then still have 160-170 yards to the green.

"Don't pull that shot, because it will roll down a hill into the hazard," advises Ron Hallett. If you push it, there is a pot bunker to catch a lot of balls.

The green slopes downhill to the left and has more break than you would think.

During the New England PGA Championships in 1991, Hallett kept a scoring average on the hole: 6.05 overall, with the scores getting better after Hurricane Bob knocked down a bunch of trees.

Olde Barnstable Fairgrounds
1991: Marstons Mills/420-1141

Architect: Brian Silva, Mark Mungeam
Course Rating: 70.8 **Course Slope:** 123
Course Record: 4-under 67 by Mike Haberl (noncompetitive); 2-under 69 (competitive) by Mike McBroom, Bruce Murphy, Ed Kirby, Mickey Herron, and Mike Haberl
Tee Time Policy: Two days in advance (up to one year, if prepaid)
Amenities: Motor carts & pull carts, alcohol bar, food service
The Skinny: Becoming one of *the* top town-owned courses on the Cape & Islands.
Directions: From the Sagamore Bridge, take Route 6 east to Exit 5. From the exit, turn right onto Route 149 south. Bear right at Prospect Street.
About 1 mile from Exit 5, you will find Olde Barnstable Fairgrounds on your left.

The Course

This is the newest course on the Cape & Islands, and some judge it as one of *the* premier town-owned courses.

Architects Brian Silva and Mark Mungeam designed the layout in what head professional Gary Philbrick calls "the old classical style." Not a long course – 6,500 yards from the back tees and 6,100 from the front – Olde Barnstable Fairgrounds still offers a lot of deception.

For example, the bunkers on some holes are 30 yards in front of the green. You think that all you must do is clear the bunker, and you'll be on the green. When you go up, however, you find that there's still 20 *more* yards to the putting surface.

Another unique feature on several of the holes is the chipping area that makes the green look bigger than it is. As if that weren't enough, Philbrick notes that some 14 of their greens are

Hol	Par	Yds	Hcp
1	5	505	9
2	3	165	17
3	5	520	6
4	5	196	13
5	4	395	3
6	4	372	15
7	4	457	1
8	4	338	11
9	4	406	7
Out	36	3,359	
10	5	520	6
11	4	348	14
12	3	176	18
13	4	356	12
14	4	396	10
15	3	196	8
16	4	412	4
17	3	185	16
18	5	560	2
In	35	3,141	
Tot	71	6,500	

undulating, so you have to know how to putt in order to fashion a good round here.

Generally speaking, difficult-to-putt greens hold up play; however, that's just not happening at Olde Barnstable. Philbrick reports that 47,000 rounds were played during its first season; more than 50,000 in its second.

"It plays pretty quickly," says Philbrick, "about 2½ hours to play the front 9 and another 2 hours on the back."

Although the course is the newest, it already has a few good stories. One concerns assistant professional Michael Haberl, a long-hitter who is the son of Dennis Pines' head pro, Jay Haberl.

Haberl was playing the 8th hole, a 338-yard par-4, which plays around a conservation area, when he cut the corner, hoping to get near the green. When they reached the green, they couldn't find Haberl's ball. So, he walked back to the tee and hit another drive.

When they returned to the green, another player went to the hole to take out the pin. Up popped Haberl's first ball. He had a hole-in-one on this par-4.

7th HOLE

The Challenge

This is a bear. A par-4 of 457 yards, it is the No. 1 stroke hole, and it plays that hard.

There is a fairway bunker 250 yards off the tee that big hitters have to worry about clearing.

Assorted bunkers protect the unusually-shaped green: long and flat, horizontally. It must be about 150 feet wide, but it is very narrow.

What happens oft-times is that somebody will hit a wood to the green, then the ball will roll through the green into a deceptive back bunker.

"Most of the players here come up short with their second shot," says Gary Philbrick. "Then they try to get up and down with a wedge for a par."

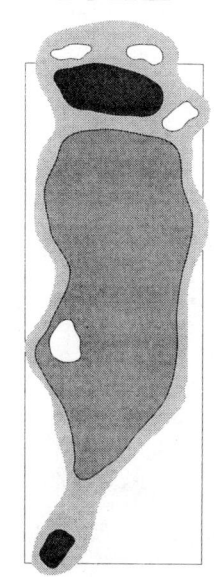

Otis

1964: Bourne/968-6453

Architect: Robert Baldock, Henry Mitchell
Course Rating: 70.8 **Course Slope:** 122
Course Record: 5-under 67 by Jack Sances (non-competitive); 3-under 69 by Ron Clark (competitive)
Tee Time Policy: Open only to golfers with military identification.
Amenities: Motor carts & pull carts, alcohol bar, food service

The Skinny: Find someone in the military so that you can play here.
Directions: From the Bourne Bridge, take Route 28 south. At the Otis Rotary follow signs into military base, where personnel at the military guardhouse will direct authorized players to the golf course.

The Course

"This may be the best kept secret on Cape Cod," admits John Callahan, a civilian who runs the golf course at the Otis Military Base. Volunteer military personnel built the original 9-hole course in 1964. Then, when the military facility closed in the early 1970s, the course nearly went fallow.

That's when Richard Iwazsko revitalized the project.

Plans to improve the course in the 1970s were drawn by Robert Baldock, a California architect who had designed several courses at military bases and veterans' hospitals; however, it was local architect Henry Mitchell, who built the 9 holes that exist today. Since then, Iwazsko has moved on to become the director of golf at nearby Pocasset Golf Club.

Still, things keep improving at Otis.

Callahan attended several architecture seminars

Hol	Par	Yds	Hcp
1	4	351	15
2	5	502	9
3	3	142	17
4	4	370	13
5	3	217	7
6	4	424	3
7	4	398	5
8	5	510	11
9	4	441	1
Out	36	3,307	
10	4	351	15
11	5	502	9
12	3	142	17
13	4	370	13
14	3	217	7
15	4	424	3
16	4	398	5
17	5	510	11
18	4	441	1
In	36	3,307	
Tot	72	6,614	

and is in the midst of designing a second 9 at the military installation.

"The original 9 is rather flat," he says. "The new 9 is being built on a piece of land with varying topography, and I hope to use a lot of the changes in elevation."

Meanwhile, if you're the sort of golfer who draws the ball, you will have an easier time at Otis than someone who fades. The best way to play this course is to drive your ball to the left side of the fairway. The exception is the 9th hole, where white out-of-bounds markers line the left side.

There are no water holes on this course; however, there are 36 sand bunkers, an inordinate amount for a 9-hole layout.

Otis is only open to military personnel. Any military officer, military retiree or dependent with a military identification card can play and bring three guests.

9th HOLE

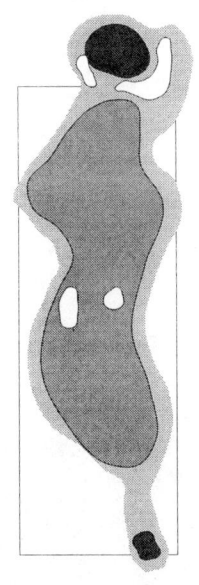

The Challenge

You have a tough tee shot on this one, a dogleg to the right that plays 441 yards. It is the No. 1 stroke hole on the golf course.

From the tee, you can see a pair of fairway bunkers in the distance. They seem to cover the fairway. The landing area is about 18 yards wide, says John Callahan. Big hitters can drive it over the right bunker. If you hit it over the left bunker, you are in trouble. It drops off into the tree line, and you'll be hitting your next shot from the woods.

Further along, there are 2 more bunkers protecting the green. If you want to run a shot up, there is a 20-yard gap to aim for. The bunker on the right is huge and curls around the right side of the green.

Just hope that the pin placement isn't in the front right. If you have a downhill putt there, it could roll right off the green.

Oyster Harbors

1927: Osterville/428-9881

Architect: Donald Ross
Course Rating: 72.8 **Course Slope:** 131
Course Record: 8-under 64 by Ken Venturi, 7-under 65 by Paul Heffernan
Tee Time Policy: Private course
Amenities: Motor carts, alcohol bar, food service
The Skinny: These are *the best* Ross bunkers in N.E.
Directions: From the Sagamore Bridge, take Route 6 east to Exit 5. From the exit, turn right onto Route 149, then bear right on Prospect Street. You'll pass Olde Barnstable Fairgrounds, then cross Race Lane. A little more than ½ mile later, the road forks: Prospect Street/Route 149 bears right, but you bear left onto Flint Street. As Flint winds, it crosses Old Falmouth Road and becomes Osterville/West Barnstable Road, then comes to a traffic light at Route 28. Crossing Route 28, this road ends at Main Street in Osterville.

Turn left on Main to the flagpole at the west end of town, then go right on Parker Road. About ¼ mile beyond, take your next right onto West Bay Road, which winds down to Bridge Street and on to Oyster Harbors. Unless you are a guest, though, you will not get past the guardhouse at Grand Island.

The Course

Oyster Harbors might be *the* most exclusive course on Cape Cod, Nantucket & Martha's Vineyard. And it might well be one of the best, too.

Formerly Grand Island, Oyster Harbors was owned by five prominent Boston families who not only developed it, but also had the wisdom to hire Donald Ross in the 1920s to build a golf course. That course and the surrounding property belonged to the Mellon family until the late 1980s. At that time, it sold the property and golf course to the Oyster Harbors membership.

The toughest stretch of holes on this layout is the 8th through the 11th, a difficult string of par-4s with the par-3 10th sandwiched between. Most of those holes are played into the prevailing south-westerly wind.

Of the entire course, the most difficult hole to putt is the 2nd, a reachable par-5 of 480 yards. The

Hol	Par	Yds	Hcp
1	4	410	5
2	5	472	13
3	3	145	17
4	5	512	3
5	3	199	15
6	4	399	1
7	4	375	9
8	4	392	7
9	4	354	11
Out	36	3,258	
10	3	206	16
11	4	437	4
12	4	396	12
13	4	401	6
14	5	542	2
15	4	407	10
16	5	457	14
17	3	174	18
18	4	411	8
In	36	3,429	
Tot	72	6,687	

green slopes right-to-left, with a mound on the right. If you miss the green to the right, you are indeed in trouble. There is no way to get up and down if the pin is on that side of the green.

Throughout its own distinguished history, Oyster Harbors has been the site of several golfing exhibitions. After Francis Ouimet won the State Open here in 1932, six more State Opens were held over the next ten years at Oyster Harbors. PGA pros Harold McSpaden and Horton Smith combined for four of those titles. In 1960, Michael Cestone defeated David Ross here for the United States Golf Association's Senior Amateur Championship.

In addition, what a list of notables it is who have walked these fairways: Gene Sarazen was a familiar guest of financier William Danforth, who also played host over the years to many golfing celebrities.

Oyster Harbors is also the home course of Joe Keller, the 1993 Massachusetts Golf Association Player-of-the-Year and two-time State Mid-Amateur Champion.

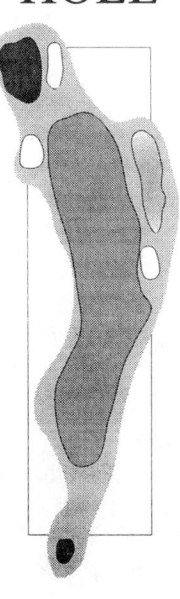

6th HOLE

The Challenge

Dick Stimets likes this 399-yard par-4, because Donald Ross liked it. "When I was a boy," he says, "I caddied for Ross here, and he told me so."

Called "Waterdog," the 6th is a dogleg left with a fairway bunker at the far end of the dogleg's elbow. If you hit beyond the dogleg, there is a pond to catch your errant shots.

Only a long hitter can take off some of the tree line. If the prevailing wind is blowing from the left to right on the tee, it will be a longer approach shot.

Your approach is anywhere from 160 yards to 200 yards. A deceptive bunker sits 40 yards short of the green, while a greenside bunker protects the right of the green.

Meanwhile, the green itself is relatively easy.

Paul Harney

1968: N. Falmouth/563-3454

Architect: Paul Harney
Course Record: 8-under 51 by Paul Harney (1977)
Course Rating: **Course Slope:**
Tee Time Policy: First come, first play
Amenities: Motor carts & pull carts, snack bar
The Skinny: Keep the ball out of the valley and you will have a good score.
Directions: From the Bourne Bridge, take Route 28 south to Route 151. Follow Route 151 nearly 4 miles past Ballymeade and Cape Cod Country Club, then Paul Harney Golf Course will be on your left.

The Course

Not long after winning the Massachusetts State Open nearby at The Country Club of New Seabury in 1967, Paul Harney was in this Hatchville section of Falmouth designing a par-3 layout. In fact, when the course first opened, it was known as the Ashumuth Valley Golf Club; however, everyone called it "Paul Harney's course," and the name stuck.

"This is a great little track," notes Cape Cod golf writer Geoff Converse of this vastly underrated layout. "If you took a regulation course and put it in the washer 'til it shrinks, it would look like the Paul Harney Golf Club."

Just because holes are shorter than a regulation course doesn't mean this is easy. In fact, you'll need all the shots if you're going to score well on this executive layout.

"The hole than gives me the most trouble is our

Hol	Par	Yds	Hcp
1	4	285	15
2	3	140	17
3	3	160	5
4	3	215	1
5	3	155	13
6	3	190	2
7	4	260	11
8	3	160	9
9	3	165	6
Out	29	1,730	
10	3	175	3
11	3	225	4
12	3	140	12
13	3	100	18
14	4	275	16
15	4	270	10
16	3	160	8
17	3	170	7
18	4	255	14
In	30	1,600	
Tot	59	3,330	

smallest: the 13th," says Mike Harney of the 100-yard challenge. "It's a feel shot. You have to hit the green; if you don't, you will roll down the hill."

Meanwhile, the string of holes that Harney and many of the club's members like the most is the 13th through the 15th.

"Those holes just feel nice to play," said Harney, but the same holds true of this whole course.

When Harney built it, he was the head professional at Pleasant Valley Country Club in Sutton, Massachusetts, so his father ran the course for the first ten years. When he moved permanently to Hatchville in the 1970s, Paul started the first golf school anywhere on Cape Cod, Nantucket & Martha's Vineyard.

To this day, when you play through the Ashumuth Valley, chances are you will not only see the former PGA Tour star operating the course with his family, but also practicing his game. He still manages to get in a quick 18, setting the course record with a sterling 8-under 51, while his sons, Michael and Tim both play this course well, too. Each has carded a 54 for these 18 holes.

4th HOLE

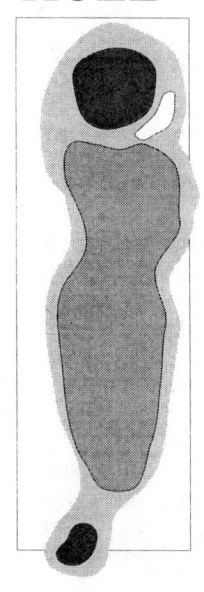

The Challenge

"You have to hit the green if you want to make a par on this hole," says Mike Harney.

Once a par-4, this has been changed to a challenging par-3; however, it's the toughest on the course. It is a long 215 yards, because it is uphill.

"You have to keep it to the left," warns Mike. "If you hit it right, you'll wind up in the dungeon."

If you pull your drive too far to the left, you can wind up in heavily-wooded trouble.

A sand bunker on the right front protects the green.

"If the superintendent is in a nasty mood," Mike adds, "he puts the pin on the right side of the green. There are going to be a lot of bogeys when he does that."

The green slopes slightly from right-to-left, but it is fairly flat. The trouble is just getting there.

Plymouth

1908: Plymouth/746-0476

Architect: Donald Ross
Course Rating: 69.0 **Course Slope:** 119
Course Record: 5-under 64 by Greg Denehy
Tee Time Policy: Call in advance for limited public access
Amenities: Motor carts & pull carts, alcohol bar, food service
The Skinny: Don't think too far ahead on any holes. Every shot can cause big numbers.
Directions: From the Sagamore Bridge, take Route 3 north; however, there is there is *no* Exit 4 in this direction. Though you can take Exit 3, the best thing to do is drive *north* to Exit 5, re-enter Route 3 *south*, then take Exit 4. This exit actually is a fork to the left from Route 3 that is named The Plimoth Plantation Highway. Follow this route about 2 miles to its junction with Route 3A.

Keep your eyes open, because the Plymouth Country Club is *immediately* on your right at this junction.

The Course

Simply put, Plymouth Country Club is one of the best seashore courses ever designed by Donald Ross. During its early years there were some 27 holes here; however, some were sold off as house lots, and others were lost when the state constructed Route 3A. So many good holes still remain at Plymouth, that it is difficult to judge the best.

The par-4 11th and par-4 12th holes are probably the toughest back-to-back holes in the area. The 11th is a slight dogleg to the left with bunkers strategically placed to deter good golfers. The 12th requires a perfect tee shot and a difficult approach to a narrow green.

The 15th through 18th are wonderful finishing holes. The 15th is a par-3 that requires a mid- to long-iron to a severely-sloped green; the 16th is a tough par-5 to an elevated green; the 17th may be the best hole on the course, a dogleg left with more

Hol	Par	Yds	Hcp
1	4	345	12
2	4	406	6
3	3	215	14
4	4	400	2
5	4	390	10
6	4	290	16
7	4	345	8
8	3	140	18
9	4	411	4
Out	34	2,942	
10	3	175	15
11	4	425	3
12	4	442	1
13	4	330	13
14	4	380	7
15	3	185	17
16	5	510	11
17	4	395	5
18	4	382	9
In	35	3,222	
Tot	69	6,164	

trouble than an Indiana Jones movie; and on the 18th, the wind tosses your ball into all sorts of trouble.

Earlier on in your round, you'll find that the 4th hole is formidable when you have to clear a chasm with your approach shot to the green. This was originally the 1st hole when Ross designed the course in 1908, and it was probably one of the toughest starting holes around. Today, they use the 4th hole as the starting hole every June for the Hornblower Memorial Tournament, one of *the* premier amateur events in New England. Players come from as far away as New York to compete in this championship.

The course is steeped in history other than the involvement of Donald Ross. Henry Picard, who won the Masters Tournament in 1938, began as a caddie at this wonderful links course. Another player who recently made a bid for the PGA Tour was Bill Buttner, who learned his skills at Plymouth.

Though Plymouth is a private course, it does permit a limited amount of public play.

17th HOLE — *The Challenge*

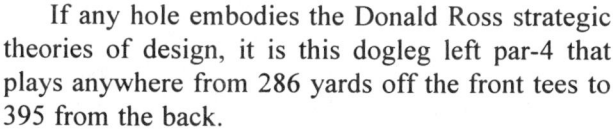

If any hole embodies the Donald Ross strategic theories of design, it is this dogleg left par-4 that plays anywhere from 286 yards off the front tees to 395 from the back.

A well-positioned drive is absolutely necessary, but then you need a perfect second shot. Long hitters won't hit a driver off the tee. They will take a fairway wood or an iron, then hit straight out to the top of the hill. The second shot can be anywhere from 150 to 200 yards.

If you must miss the green with your approach shot, miss it short. Though a stream runs through, you will have an uphill chip. Leave your chip beneath the hole.

Like most Ross greens, this one is treacherous. Many times you see a break that isn't there. You play the break, but the putt goes straight. If that happens, you've been *Ross*ed!

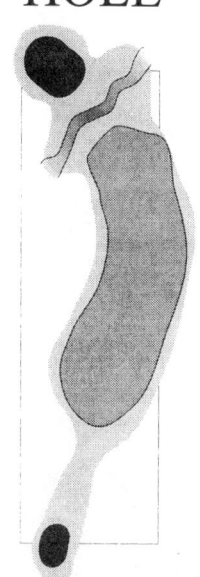

Pocasset

1916: Pocasset/563-7171

Architect: Donald Ross, (r) Manny Francis, Steve Carr, Tony Paganis
Course Rating: 70.2 **Course Slope:** 120
Course Record: 6-under 66 by Bob Prophett (non-competitive); 4-under 68s have been carded by several golfers over the years in competitive play
Tee Time Policy: Private course
Amenities: Motor carts, alcohol bar, food service

The Skinny: You'd better have your putting stroke when you come here.
Directions: From the Bourne Bridge, take Route 28 south about 3 miles, then turn right onto Barlows Landing Road. About 2 miles along, turn left onto County Road and drive another mile to Clubhouse Drive on the right, where you will find Pocasset.

The Course

Ever since the turn of the century, there has been a golf course in the Pocasset area; however, the Pocasset Golf Club that exists today began in 1916, when a wealthy group of landowners brought in Donald Ross to design an 18-hole course.

This would become the first of many visits to the Cape & Islands by Ross to build, expand, or reconstruct championship golf courses.

John I. Taylor of the *Boston Globe* publishing family purchased the course, then a group that included Massachusetts Judge Vincent Brogna later took over the club. William Carr purchased the course in 1948 before he sold it to a group of members in 1989 who made Pocasset a private course once again.

Though they call this layout a Donald Ross design, many architects have added to the track over the years. In fact, the original clubhouse is no

Hol	Par	Yds	Hcp
1	5	470	7
2	4	459	1
3	3	162	17
4	4	323	15
5	4	335	13
6	3	187	9
7	4	372	11
8	4	383	3
9	5	494	5
Out	36	3,185	
10	4	318	10
11	4	385	6
12	3	111	18
13	4	300	16
14	4	360	8
15	3	135	14
16	5	490	12
17	5	533	4
18	4	408	2
In	36	3,040	
Tot	72	6,225	

longer even near the course, but a long par-5 away from the property. It had been on the other side of the railroad tracks that border the present club property along the 3rd and 4th holes. Only the 1st and 18th holes had been on that other side.

To keep the struggling course alive in the 1950s and 1960s, however, William Carr sold that land and developed housing. Architects Manny Francis and Carr's son, Steven, who serves as greens superintendent, built some new holes and redirected others.

Member Tony Paganis is a golf course builder who also has done some of Pocasset's bunkering work, most noticeably on the opening hole.

During all that reconstruction, Pocasset lost some great holes, including the old 10th and 18th holes. The 18th was an interesting par-4 with a gulch of scrub pines and a horrific waste area that big-hitters tried to drive over. When Gary Player was on hand in 1964 for the 50th anniversary of the Cape Cod Canal, he drove that 18th green.

2nd HOLE

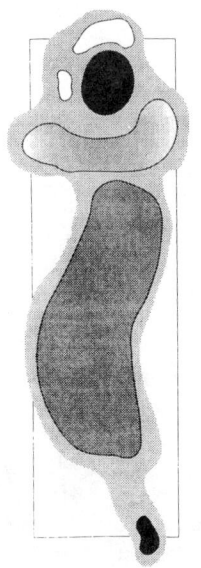

The Challenge

Donald Ross did not design this monster 459-yard par-4; however, it is an amalgamation of 2 of his holes: a short par-3 and a par-4. As with most holes on the Cape & Islands, the wind *always* plays a factor.

It is usually blowing in your face when you stand on the tee. You can hit a driver. In fact, you *must* if you want to reach this hole in 2 shots.

The sloping fairway, which helps your drive, makes the second shot tricky. Pocasset's director of golf, Rich Iwaszko, says he's hit everything from a driver to a 7-iron for his second shot.

You can't be fearless with your approach shot. If you miss it, there is a pond that fronts the green and collects many errant drives. Two bunkers protect the green, which does not have much slope. The putting surface is unprotected, so when the wind dries it out, the surface is sneaky fast.

Quashnet Valley

1976: Mashpee/477-4412

Architect: Geoffrey Cornish, William G. Robinson, Phil Wogan
Course Rating: 68.3 **Course Slope:** 125
Course Record: 3-under 69 by Jim Ruschioni (1987), Andy Morse (1989), Joe Keller (1993)
Tee Time Policy: One week in advance
Amenities: Motor carts & pull carts, alcohol bar, food service

The Skinny: You have to stay in the fairway if you are going to score.
Directions: From the Bourne Bridge, take Route 28 south to Route 151. Follow Route 151 east, passing Ballymeade, Cape Cod Country Club, and Paul Harney's, to the Falmouth/Mashpee town line.
About 1 mile after the town line, you will come to the intersection of Route 151 with Old Barnstable Road. Turn left onto Old Barnstable Road to Quashnet Valley.

The Course

Quashnet Valley opened as a 9-hole golf course in 1975, then it nearly went under during the controversial land claims presented by Mashpee's Wampanoag Indian tribe in the early 1980s. During that period, developer Tony LaCava took a chance and purchased the course. When the court later ruled in favor of the current land-owners, LaCava won his gamble. Then he hired Geoffrey Cornish to build a second 9 in 1985.

Now, if you are going to have a good round at Quashnet Valley, you'd better hit the ball straight. There are abandoned cranberry bogs, and 10 holes have water hazards of one kind or another. They can all give you a big number very quickly.

The front 9 is the newer of the two, and it has proven to be a penal 9. Quashnet Valley's head professional, Bob Chase, says that there was a time when an expert player couldn't hit a driver on *any*

Hol	Par	Yds	Hcp
1	5	505	1
2	3	125	17
3	4	326	13
4	4	310	9
5	3	153	15
6	4	420	3
7	5	488	5
8	3	173	11
9	4	349	7
Out	35	2,839	
10	4	302	14
11	4	390	6
12	4	322	16
13	5	530	4
14	4	354	10
15	4	360	8
16	4	339	12
17	3	145	18
18	5	480	2
In	37	3,521	
Tot	72	6,360	

hole on the front 9; however, that's all changed. Chase and architect Phil Wogan made some changes to the front so that now a good player can use his driver on 3 of the 9 holes. Plus, it gives the average player a more forgiving and wider landing area.

For example, the 1st hole at Quashnet was once *the* toughest starting hole on the Cape & Islands. Too severe, the fairway was only 30 feet wide with out-of-bounds to the left, as well as a bog along the right. Chase has since doubled the width of the fairway.

The 6th hole had been an *impossible* hole to play. This 430-yard par-4 had a fairway bunker in the middle of the landing area for your tee shot. After that, there was a tree in the middle of the fairway about 90 yards from the green. Chase and Wogan removed the tree, then moved the fairway bunker to the side.

The 7th hole was another tight driving hole with water down the left side and a ditch along the right. So, they filled the ditch to enlarge the landing area.

"It's a fun place to play now," says Chase.

11th HOLE

The Challenge

Bob Chase calls this hole the most under-rated hole on the course. And those who have traveled to Mashpee to play Quashnet Valley, know the 11th can spell trouble.

It plays 401 yards from the championship tees to 305 yards from the front tees.

If you block your drive to the right, there is a hill dotted with the Cape's trademark scrub pines. Either your ball will hide in the high brush or roll down the hill into the fairway. If your tee shot strays left, you may *never* find it, because it is in a hazard: an abandoned cranberry bog. So, you go to the point of entry and take your penalty stroke.

If you don't hit a perfect drive, your second shot can be a long iron to an elevated green, which has a subtle break from back-to-front. Well-placed bunkers on both the left and right protect the green, and there is a bunker behind the green as well.

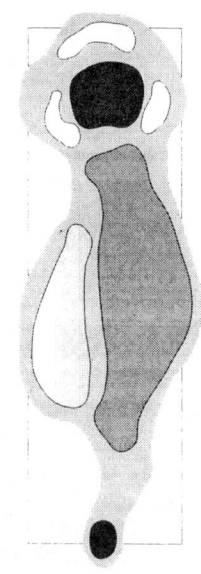

Ridge Club

1990: S. Sandwich/428-6800

Architect: Robert von Hagge
Course Rating: 72.6 **Course Slope:** 132
Course Record: 1-under 70 by John Boniface (gold)
Tee Time Policy: Private course
Amenities: Motor carts & pull carts, alcohol bar, food service
The Skinny: There are plenty of heroic shots at this course.

Directions: From the Sagamore Bridge, take Route 6 east to Exit 3. From the exit, turn right onto Quaker Meetinghouse Road south, and drive to the traffic lights that intersect with Cotuit Road. Turn left onto Cotuit Road, then take your first left onto Farmersville Road.

You will pass signs for Holly Ridge on your right, then come to The Ridge Club further along on the right.

The Course

The Ridge Club is unlike anything else on Cape Cod, Nantucket & Martha's Vineyard. For that matter, *nothing* else resembles it in New England, except perhaps the Tournament Players Club in River Highlands, Connecticut.

Nationally recognized architect Robert von Hagge, a former Naval Academy midshipman, artist, and PGA Tour player, designed this layout. He had assisted Dick Wilson in the creation of Bay Hill in Florida and of Moon Valley in Arizona. Later, he joined PGA star Bruce Devlin and was the architect of TPC Woodlands in Texas, as well as El Conquistador in Puerto Rico. Together, they also built several courses in Japan, Australia, France, and Mexico.

The sandy-based landscape in South Sandwich permitted von Hagge to move 500,000 cubic feet of earth in shaping The Ridge Club. As a result,

Hol	Par	Yds	Hcp
1	4	351	11
2	3	131	17
3	5	495	3
4	4	349	13
5	4	372	7
6	4	374	9
7	3	177	15
8	4	395	1
9	4	389	5
Out	35	3,033	
10	4	375	10
11	3	182	16
12	5	59	4
13	4	382	2
14	3	167	18
15	5	581	12
16	4	398	6
17	3	139	14
18	5	529	8
In	36	3,249	
Tot	71	6,282	

dramatic and varied mounds are commonplace on every hole; however, they are not placed there in a haphazard manner. On the contrary, they not only guide the golfer around, but also conceal more than five miles of cart paths throughout The Ridge.

Because you get a different look each time you play this course, you won't ever be bored. *Each hole* has anywhere from 4 to 7 teeing areas. In play are 2 natural ponds, plus 4 man-made water retention areas.

The 3 finishing holes are spectacular, and they can be seen regularly on the televised broadcasts of the *Tucker Anthony Classic*. The 16th is a dogleg right par-4 of 380 yards; the par-3 17th is an island green that plays anywhere from 156 to 100 yards; and the 18th hole is a gambler's dream. You can get home in 2 if you have a good drive; however, you must clear a 12 *million* gallon pond between the fairway and the green.

1st HOLE

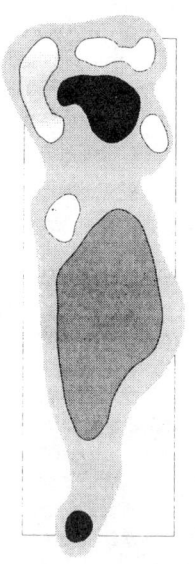

The Challenge

A short par-4 of 330 yards from the middle tees, this is Tom Niblet's pride. "It is one of my favorites," he says, "because of its natural beauty."

You can hit your tee shot out there 175 yards to a fairway terrace, from which the green is some 70 feet below with a pond to its left. Because of that sudden drop in elevation, as well as the wind, picking the correct club for your second shot is a real trick.

If you are a gambler or a long hitter, you can try to bust a drive. Then, hope it bounces down the hill and onto the green. If you pull your tee shot left, however, you can wind up out-of-bounds or in a bunker. And if you push your round-opening drive to the right, you are in the wilderness.

There is a pond to the left of the green, which is huge and susceptible to 3-putting. Bunkers sit behind, as well as to the right.

Round Hill

1971: Sandwich/888-3384

Architect: Sam Volpe, Richard Cross
Course Rating: 70.4 **Course Slope:** 124
Course Record: 5-under 66 by Bruce Murphy (1988)
Tee Time Policy: One week in advance
Amenities: Motor carts & pull carts, alcohol bar, food service
The Skinny: It isn't difficult. Just don't try any miraculous shots.

Directions: From the Sagamore Bridge, take Route 6 east to Exit 3. From the exit turn right onto Quaker Meetinghouse Road, then take your *very first* left onto the service road that runs parallel to Route 6. About ½ mile along the service road, you will find Round Hill on the right.

The Course

Not long after he had erected the hangers at nearby Otis military base, contractor Sam Volpe hired an architect to design and build these 18 holes in 1971. As the first 9 neared completion, however, Volpe was furious, because the architect already had spent on 9 holes as much as Volpe had intended to spend for all 18. So, he fired the architect and built the others on his own.

The architect disassociated himself from the project altogether, and that was a huge mistake on Volpe's part. He did not know anything about golf architecture, and the result was appalling. The 9 holes designed by the architect proved playable; however, the 9 that Volpe built simply were not.

After the completion of the golf course, Volpe died. He was interred in a mausoleum upon a hill near the 18th tee, one of the highest points of the peninsula on the Sandwich Moraine. Then his wife

Hol	Par	Yds	Hcp
1	5	495	9
2	4	334	11
3	3	128	17
4	4	310	15
5	4	362	3
6	5	595	7
7	3	185	5
8	4	350	13
9	4	420	1
Out	36	3,179	
10	4	320	18
11	4	390	6
12	3	195	12
13	4	292	14
14	4	550	8
15	3	171	10
16	4	350	16
17	4	365	2
18	4	345	4
In	35	3,179	
Tot	71	6,157	

ordered a stand of magnificent trees cut down so that she could always see his resting place from the clubhouse. Shortly thereafter, she died too and was buried in the same mausoleum beside the 18th tee, now called Chapel Hill.

In the mid-1980s, the Striar family purchased the golf course, which also happens to be one of the largest parcels of land in the Town of Sandwich. In 1986, Soozen Striar took over as the general manager, and since then she has worked to change Round Hill's image and to make the course more playable.

"Even today, I'll go somewhere and people find out I run Round Hill. Then they tell me they tried playing Round Hill and it was not a fair golf course," says Striar. "So I give them a free pass. I tell them to play it again and see the changes for themselves."

No doubt, people recognize the improvements.

9th HOLE

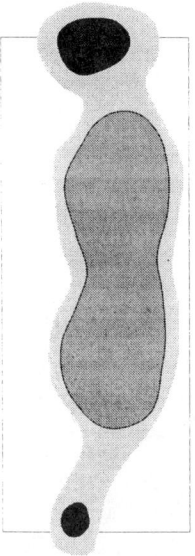

The Challenge

What makes this hole so difficult is that the distance for your approach shot to the green is deceptive. So much so, in fact, that head pro John Lyons notes that few golfers ever hit enough club.

This straightaway par-4 plays 420 yards from the back tees to 309 from the front. It is also the No. 1 stroke hole, the most difficult of the course.

The fairway rises, then dips. There are trees down the right side and out-of-bounds on the left. They cut the elevated green into the side of a hill, 25 feet above the fairway. It is a monster with the wind seemingly always in your face.

"If you are at the 150-yard marker, you are thinking 7-iron; however, you will never get there with that," says Lyons.

If you miss the green to the left or the right, the hill will deflect it into an abyss. Bogey will be a good recovery.

Sankaty Head

1923: Siasconset/257-6655

Architect: Skip Wogan, A.W. Tillinghast
Course Rating: 70.6 **Course Slope:** 128
Course Record: 7-under 65 by Peter Morgan (1993)
Tee Time Policy: Private course
Amenities: Caddies, golf carts, alcohol bar, food service
The Skinny: Don't get caught up in the beauty if you want a good round.

Directions: From Hyannis or Woods Hole, you can take a ferry to Nantucket. From the head of Main Street, travel easterly on Orange Street to the traffic rotary at the Milestone Road. Follow Milestone Road east to the village of Siasconset. Just past the water pump at the center of the village, turn left onto Sankaty Avenue, which will lead you to Sankaty Head Golf Links.

The Course

Sankaty Head is one of the true links courses to be enjoyed in America. Resembling ocean waves whenever the southwesterly breezes blow across the island, Sankaty's high rough is similar to the heather that can only be found in Scotland. With but a few trees and but 1 water hole on the links, the constant wind that sweeps over Nantucket significantly changes the conditions and how you play the course.

Skip Wogan created Sankaty Head. An early associate of Ross, Wogan was one of the founders of the New England PGA. A.W. Tillinghast, the great architect from Philadelphia, had a hand in this design, too. Clearly, it is one of New England's most scenic courses with the view of the majestic ocean and the presence of Sankaty Head Light.

Just as the Highland Golf Links at North Truro sits atop a glacial moraine on the peninsula, so does

Hol	Par	Yds	Hcp
1	4	388	11
2	4	375	5
3	3	193	9
4	5	477	13
5	4	421	1
6	3	168	15
7	4	393	3
8	5	502	7
9	4	289	17
Out	36	3,206	
10	4	424	2
11	5	474	16
12	3	197	12
13	4	378	6
14	3	136	18
15	4	398	4
16	4	388	8
17	5	486	14
18	4	378	10
In	36	3,259	
Tot	72	6,465	

Sankaty Head sit upon one of the higher points of this island. Reason enough for both of them to have lighthouses nearby.

Because Sankaty Head is unprotected from the elements, the greens are even faster than they appear. As if that were not enough, they are also small and dreadfully, well-bunkered.

In a turn-of-the-century mindset, Sankaty's holes are not only numbered, but also named. You begin with *Outward Bound*, a 388-yard par-4; then you play *Pocomo, Quidnet, Sesachacha, Light Apoint, Pine Valley, Cross Rip, Come About,* and *Gray Lady* for the front 9. The back 9 is no less quaint with: *Carry On, High Knoll, Westward Ho, Coffin's Corner, Wee One, Light Ahoy, Round the Horn, Long Journey,* and *Thar She Blows!*

During the summer months, they do restrict the use of the course to members and their guests. Guests must play with a member.

Sankaty Head remains the site of the only existing caddie camp in New England. They say it is more difficult to get into the caddie camp than it is to become a Sankaty Head member.

5th HOLE

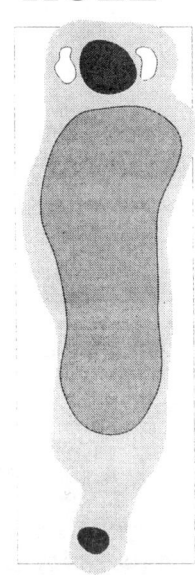

The Challenge

They call this 421-yard par-4 *Light Aport*, meaning there is a lighthouse on the left. The highest elevation on the golf course, the back tee of this hole gives a majestic view of the Atlantic, the lighthouse, and the charming village of Siasconset (pronounced simply *'Sconset*).

In the distance is a directional flag.

"Just aim at the flag and hit it straight," says assistant pro Andrew Campbell. "However, be weary of the wind." The prevailing wind is right-to-left, and if you hit a draw you can land in the ample rough.

The approach shot is downhill to a bowl-shaped green, which has treacherous bunkers on both sides, as well as a penal high rough and scrub oak to frame it. The most difficult green to putt at Sankaty Head, this one is sloped steeply from back-to-front.

Seaside Links

1914: Chatham/945-4774

Architect: Original owner Charles Hardy
Course Rating: 61.8 **Course Slope:** 102
Course Record: 7-under 61 by George Hill (1956)
Tee Time Policy: First come, first to play
Amenities: Pull carts, rental clubs, pro shop
The Skinny: A fun place that doesn't take too long to play.
Directions: From the Sagamore Bridge, take Route 6 east to Exit 11. From the exit, turn left onto Route 137. Follow this road past the traffic lights at the intersection with Route 139, beyond the lights at the intersection with Queen Anne Road, and all the way to its end at Route 28.

Turn left on Route 28 and travel 3½ miles to the center of Chatham, where this road is Main Street. Just beyond the traffic rotary, take your first left uphill onto Sea View Street. You will come to Seaside Links.

The Course

If you're on vacation with someone who wants to learn the game, Seaside Links is a wonderful place to begin.

Though relatively open, this is not a long course. The rolling fairways are dry during the summer months, and you will get extra distance, even from a mis-hit shot. The beginning golfer will have a chance to get that confidence-building par or even the elusive birdie. For example, the 3rd hole, a 130-yard par-3, becomes just such an opportunity as you hit an iron onto an inviting green.

In a few areas, such as the 7th and 8th holes, you will have to negotiate some hills; however, none of these 9 holes is a dogleg. There is water on 2 holes, and sand bunkers guard most greens, which are small. In fact, you really need a good pitch-and-run game to do well here.

The prettiest spot on the course is the 7th hole.

Hol	Par	Yds	Hcp
1	4	315	3
2	4	235	11
3	3	130	17
4	3	175	7
5	4	350	1
6	4	275	13
7	4	295	5
8	4	255	15
9	4	295	9
Out	34	2,325	
10	4	315	4
11	4	235	12
12	3	130	18
13	3	175	8
14	4	350	2
15	4	275	14
16	4	295	6
17	4	255	16
18	4	295	10
In	34	2,325	
Tot	68	4,650	

From the top of its hill, you can look over your shoulder to a panoramic view of Chatham Harbor, North Beach and the nearby Atlantic Ocean.

One of the oldest courses on the Cape & Islands, the Links was built in 1914 by Charles Hardy, the late owner and operator of the Chatham Bars Inn. Originally, some of the holes crossed both Sea View Street and Chatham Bars Avenue; however, both the changing population and the increase in traffic required that those holes no longer cross the thoroughfare.

During the 1980s golf boom, the Town of Chatham looked into building its own golf course, but chose instead to purchase the Chatham Bars course in 1989 and rename this Seaside Links.

4th HOLE

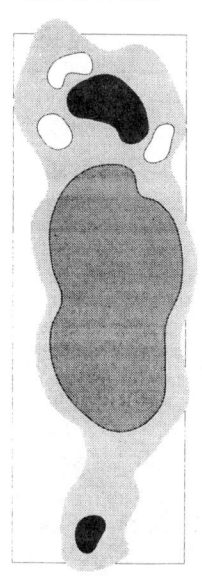

The Challenge

There are only 2 par-3 holes at Seaside Links; however, this par-3 is handicapped as the 3rd hardest of the 9 holes on the course.

It plays anywhere from 185 yards to 165 yards, and the challenge comes from its required uphill shot.

The prevailing wind is in your face so you will hit anything from a 4-iron to a wood. Most players do need more club than they first think, so take one more club that you would ordinarily use.

Bunkers to the left, to the right, and to the rear protect this small green, which doesn't hold a shot very well. Once you do get on the green, though, you will have a fairly flat putting surface.

Siasconset

1894: Siasconset/257-6596

Architect: Alex Finlay, John Grout
Course Rating: 68.1 **Course Slope:** 113
Course Record: 2-under 68 by Mike Brady
Tee Time Policy: Place your ball in the rack. First come, first place.
Amenities: Pull carts, pro shop, snack bar
The Skinny: Docile, unless the wind blows.
Directions: From Hyannis or Woods Hole, you can take a ferry to Nantucket.
From the head of Main Street, travel easterly on Orange Street to the traffic rotary at the Milestone Road. Follow Milestone Road east to the village of Siasconset.

The Course

The first golf course on Nantucket, Siasconset (pronounced *'Sconset*) was built in 1894. That also makes this island layout one of the 10 oldest courses in America, depending on whose version of history you choose to believe.

According to some publications, the architect was Alex Finlay, a Scot who worked at the Wright & Ditson Sporting Goods Store in Boston when he wasn't designing courses. According to Siasconset operator Robert (Skinner) Coffin, however, the architect was a John Grout of Detroit.

In either case, this had 18 holes. "You can still see some of the old square greens," says Coffin. "They are in a part we don't use anymore."

The greens are a reminder of the early part of this century, when many of golf's great players came to Nantucket and played here. In 1917, Boston professional Mike Brady set a record of

Hol	Par	Yds	Hcp
1	3	200	15
2	5	468	1
3	4	300	7
4	5	400	3
5	3	140	17
6	4	245	11
7	3	215	13
8	4	310	5
9	4	265	9
Out	35	2,543	
10	3	200	16
11	5	468	2
12	4	300	8
13	5	400	4
14	3	140	18
15	4	245	12
16	3	215	14
17	4	310	6
18	4	265	10
In	35	2,543	
Tot	70	5,086	

sorts. Playing with the French professional Louis Tellier and two Siasconset members, Brady scored *a pair* of holes-in-one during a single round. Brady shot a course record 68 that day; the following morning he almost surpassed his previous day's achievement until he wound up in a bunker on the 17th and took a bogey. His best ball for two days was a 12-under 58.

When Sankaty Head opened nearby in the 1920s, several of Siasconset's members joined the newer club. Since the older club didn't have many members, it cut back from 18 to 9 holes and let the rest of the course grow over. Though there are no more square greens, Coffin says that things have not really changed that much. The greens are small, the bunkers are sporadically scattered, and the hard turf lets you hit a drive a long way.

A 9-hole round takes only about 1½ hours, and Coffin caters to daily fee play. With no tee times, you simply put your ball into the ball rack. The only tournament they hold is the mid-September Skinner Open, where the Rules of Golf are all but abandoned. Players can to throw the ball twice, and they are given 3 *mulligans*.

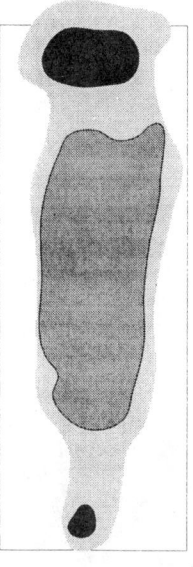

7th HOLE

The Challenge

Whenever a par-3 is the toughest hole at a golf course it can usually mean a couple of things: either it is a par-3 course, or else the par-4s are easy. This hole, however, is one *tough* par-3. It is 215 yards from the back tees and plays directly into the prevailing southwesterly wind.

Don't think of running your shot up, either.

What makes this hole so hard, says Skinner Coffin, is a ditch that runs right in front of the green and catches the ground balls.

But that isn't the only problem you will encounter.

To the right of the green are some bushes. While they are about 30 feet from the green, they seem a lot closer when the wind is blowing. They certainly catch a lot of balls.

Squirrel Run

1992: Plymouth/746-5001

Architect: Ray Richard, Jr.
Course Record: 7-under 51 by Bruce Murphy
Course Rating: 53.7 **Course Slope:** 83
Tee Time Policy: One week in advance
Amenities: Motor carts & pull carts, alcohol bar, food service
The Skinny: If you need work on your short game, not a bad place to go.

Directions: From the Sagamore Bridge, take Route 3 north to Exit 6. From the exit, turn left to the bottom of the ramp at Route 44. Turn left onto Route 44 west and drive beneath Route 3. Follow Route 44 west about 3 miles, where you will see the entrance to Squirrel Run on the left.

The Course

Slow play turned businessman Charlie Caranci away from the game.

"I hated whenever I finished a hole," he says. "I'd go to the next tee, and there would be two groups waiting to play it." Caranci, you see, is a busy man. Not the type of person who can sit still, he is a builder, a creator whose endeavors include a winery, a mobile home park, and a golf course.

His wife, Jane, had begun playing the game in 1987, only to become an avid and quickly-improving golfer. "When I needed a place to practice," she says, "he built me a driving range."

Of course, Charlie Caranci might have built a housing development on the tract of land that Squirrel Run occupies; however, when the market went soft in the late 1980s, Jane suggested that he build an executive golf course.

So, in August of 1991 they broke ground, and

Hol	Par	Yds	Hcp
1	4	310	3
2	3	131	1
3	4	140	11
4	3	120	16
5	4	270	13
6	3	120	5
7	3	153	17
8	3	170	9
9	4	230	7
Out	31	1,650	
10	3	120	8
11	3	109	4
12	3	120	15
13	3	132	18
14	3	190	12
15	3	125	14
16	3	128	2
17	3	112	6
18	3	175	10
In	27	1,201	
Tot	58	2,765	

Squirrel Run opened some fourteen months later. Others would have rushed to open this course in the summer of 1992. Some would have wanted to earn more greens fees from the golf-hungry summer population migrating toward the Cape & Islands. Caranci avoided the temptation. Blame his pride. He wanted to wait until all of the conditions were perfect.

At the northern gate to the golfing kingdom that is Cape Cod, Nantucket & Martha's Vineyard, this Plymouth layout is not a championship golf course. There are no 600-yard par-5s with 3 carries over water. There are no uphill 470-yard par-4s that only 1% of the golfing public can reach in regulation. In fact, one of the best things about this layout is that the average player can enjoy the course and the opportunity to putt for birdies.

More impressive, though, are the conditions of this layout. The tees are manicured, and the greens are always pristine.

16th HOLE *The Challenge*

This is the type of golf hole you love to hate, for it will ruin many a round of golf at this course. If you hit a good tee shot and make 2 good putts for a par, you should be happy with yourself.

Things, however, can easily go wrong.

For example, if you block your tee shot to the right, you will probably hit it over the chain-link fence. It would be out-of-bounds, and you would have to hit another tee shot.

If you pull your tee shot to the left of the green, you have a treacherous chip 15 feet below the hourglass green, which is precarious. You'd better take your time lining-up putts, because this green is as treacherous as any you will ever play. If you are above the pin, chances are you will run your first putt past the hole and wind up 3-putting.

In short, making a par on this hole is like making a birdie on any of Squirrel Run's other 17.

Tara Woods

1966: Hyannis/775-7775

Architect: Geoffrey Cornish
Course Rating: N/A **Course Slope:** N/A
Course Record: 8-under 46 by Ken Harrelson
Tee Time Policy: Two days in advance
Amenities: Pull carts, alcohol bar, food service
The Skinny: Don't hit any balls into the adjacent hotel.
Directions: From the Sagamore Bridge, take Route 6 east to Exit 6. From the exit, turn right onto Route 132 south and prepare for the next two turns. After the first set of traffic lights, stay in the right lane and bear right onto Bearse's Way. This follows behind the Cape Cod Mall for about a mile before it crosses Route 28 at a traffic light and then continues yet another mile to a light at North Street.

At North Street, turn right and follow to the West End Rotary, where the traffic circulates past West Main, Scudder Avenue, Main Street and North Street in that order. As you yield to traffic in the rotary, be aware that you will be taking your second right: Scudder Avenue. The entrance to Tara Woods is at the far end of the hotel's parking lot.

The Course

Golf Digest has called this the most challenging par-3 course on Cape Cod. You can understand why, for the holes are long with plenty of hazards, and the greens are nothing less than treacherous. In fact, for a public course with so much play, the greens here are *exceptional*. Healthy and without many blotches, they are consistent and true. If you get your putt on the correct line, it stays there!

"They are not the best greens you'll ever putt," admits head pro Fred Ghioto, "but we've had members come over from Hyannisport and claim these greens are as good as theirs."

Over the years, Tara Woods has had several names. When Geoffrey Cornish designed the course in the 1960s, they called it Fiddler's Green. Then, after the Dunfey family purchased the hotel, they changed the name simply to Dunfey's. Now that the Flatley Company owns this, it is Tara Woods.

Hol	Par	Yds	Hcp
1	3	135	6
2	3	90	18
3	3	165	4
4	3	144	12
5	3	110	14
6	3	102	16
7	3	175	2
8	3	140	10
9	3	135	8
Out	27	1,196	
10	3	190	3
11	3	140	13
12	3	150	7
13	3	115	15
14	3	170	5
15	3	215	1
16	3	150	9
17	3	160	11
18	3	135	17
In	27	1,425	
Tot	54	2,621	

Because the Cape Cod Melody Tent is directly across the street and many of the performers stay at the hotel throughout the summer, you never know who might be teeing it up. One such celebrity is former Red Sox slugger Ken Harrelson, who holds the course record with a red-hot, 8-under 46. (Harrelson also holds the course record at Ballymeade.) Tara Woods assistant professional Peter Lizotte nearly erased Harrelson's record with his 7-under 47 in 1993; however, it was a round of *what-could-have-been* since Lizotte missed a pair of 3-foot putts.

If Tara Woods isn't busy, says Ghioto, you go around these 18 holes in 2½ hours; if it is busy, maybe 3. The worst he has heard is a 4-hour round. Still, that's a *lot* better than regulation courses, where it might take 5 or 6 hours to play during the summer.

3rd HOLE

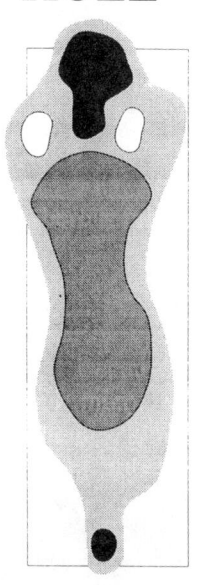

The Challenge

This 165-yard hole is *not* the No. 1 stroke hole, but it certainly will give you fits. You must hit the green, and the best way to do that is to make sure you have enough club.

"The prevailing wind is in your face," says head pro Fred Ghioto. Because of the elevated green, you might not feel it as you stand on the tee.

As if the wind were not enough, however, there is nothing but woods on the left side of this huge green, one of the biggest on the course. If you miss the green left, you are going to make a bogey. If you miss it to the right, this will become a double- or triple-bogey.

In addition, 2 bunkers protect the green, and your chances of getting a par from the bunkers are slim and none.

Meanwhile, the green itself is undulating with plenty of mounds.

White Cliffs

1961: Cedarville/888-2110

Architect: Geoffrey Cornish, Karl Litten, Gary Player
Course Rating: 60.9 **Course Slope:** 101
Course Record: 5-under 57 by John Gordon (1992)
Tee Time Policy: Private course
Amenities: Motor carts, alcohol bar, food service
The Skinny: If you are going to make birdies, it won't be on the par-3s.
Directions: From the Sagamore Bridge, take Route 3 north to Exit 2. From the exit, take a left. In less than ¼ mile, you will take a right. Signs direct you to White Cliffs, whose entrance is clearly visible to your left.

The Course

From the stretch of Route 3 that rolls north from the Sagamore Bridge, you can see 8 of White Cliffs' holes in the valley-like plot.

Geoffrey Cornish designed the original White Cliffs Golf Course back in 1961. In the mid-1980s, however, a Worcester group purchased the property and developed the White Cliffs residential community that overlooks Cape Cod Bay. After hiring PGA Senior Tour star Gary Player to design the course, the company bulldozed the old course and built an entirely new one which opened in 1986.

The 1st and 18th holes play along the high cliffs with a dramatic 130-foot drop to the beach below and a spectacular view of Cape Cod Bay. More than a few golfers have taken an old ball out of their bag and launched them from the 18th tee toward the ocean. Obviously, their shots have more hang time than a National Football League punt.

Hol	Par	Yds	Hcp
1	4	375	5
2	3	133	14
3	4	342	3
4	3	125	13
5	4	330	1
6	4	270	12
7	3	200	7
8	4	310	9
9	4	272	11
Out	33	2,357	
10	5	485	4
11	3	192	2
12	3	145	10
13	3	84	18
14	3	152	6
15	3	119	17
16	3	106	15
17	3	109	16
18	3	160	8
In	39	2,357	
Tot	62	3,909	

Just because White Cliffs is an executive course doesn't mean that this is an easy pitch-and-putt course. In fact, because the trees are growing taller, it is getting more difficult to drive those holes. So, the course requires exacting placement shots.

The 10th is a wonderful go-for-broke par-5, while both the 7th and 9th holes are short par-4s where you can gamble. You can try to drive over the trees and reach the green for an eagle putt; however, you'd better try it when the wind is with you. The day Gary Player opened the course, he did his best to drive the 9th green, only to have his ball land in the water.

In addition, there are a few devilish par-3s. In particular, the 11th requires a 190-yard carry over water; however, take more club than you think you need. The wind is always in your face.

White Cliffs also has *the* biggest green of any course on the Cape & Islands. It is really a double green for the 8th and 10th holes.

5th HOLE

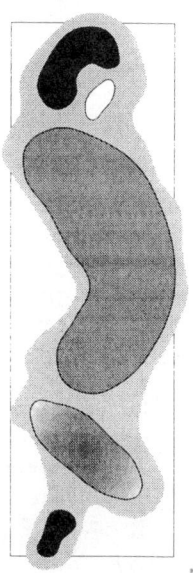

The Challenge

This hole measures only 330 yards, but yardage is not what makes the 5th the most difficult hole. The problem is footage: the putting surface.

You don't want a downhill putt on this green.

"It is *the* toughest putting surface I've seen," says pro John Gordon. "You would rather miss the green short and chip than have a downhill putt."

Think ahead to this spot. You might want to hit a fairway wood off the tee. There is out-of-bounds to the left, water to the front, and to the right is high fescue grass. With less club off the tee, you also will have a better chance of a flat lie for your approach shot. You want to leave yourself with a good angle to the green.

When they built the green, this was so severe they had to redesign it not long after the course opened. It remains such a treacherous surface that it may be reconstructed *again*.

Wianno

1916: Osterville/428-9840

Architect: Leonard Biles, (r) Donald Ross
Course Rating: 68.6 **Course Slope:** 120
Course Record: 5-under 65 by Rusty Gunnarson (competitive), 8-under by 62 Ted Turner
Tee Time Policy: Private course, not open to public
Amenities: Motor carts, alcohol bar, food service
The Skinny: Once you get on the greens, stay alert.
Directions: From the Sagamore Bridge, take Route 6 east to Exit 5. From the exit, turn right onto Route 149 south, then bear right on Prospect Street. Pass Olde Barnstable Fairgrounds and cross Race Lane.

A little more than ½ mile later, the road forks: Prospect Street/Route 149 bears right, but you want to bear left onto Flint Street. As Flint winds, it crosses Old Falmouth Road and becomes Osterville/West Barnstable Road, then comes to a traffic light at Route 28. Crossing Route 28, the road finally ends 1 mile later at Main Street in Osterville.

Turn left onto Main and follow to the flagpole at the west end of town. Go right on Parker Road. About ¼ mile beyond, take your next right onto West Bay Road, where you will find the golf course.

The Course

Wianno is unique among area golf courses, because it belongs to The Wianno Club, whose main building is a mile or so south overlooking Nantucket Sound and whose membership consists of wealthy families from throughout the United States.

After Leonard Biles designed a rudimentary course, Donald Ross came to the Cape in 1916 and expanded Wianno to 18 holes. While the result may not be the toughest golf course on Cape Cod, Nantucket & Martha's Vineyard, its excellent conditions and comfortable setting continue to make it a favorite of many.

A short course with 5 par-3s, Wianno is still not a course that many will tear up. The greens are small, and you could hit it out-of-bounds on 12 of 18 holes. Nonetheless, there are some wonderful holes at Wianno.

Hol	Par	Yds	Hcp
1	4	295	15
2	4	443	1
3	3	143	17
4	5	445	11
5	3	193	7
6	4	383	5
7	4	333	9
8	5	537	3
9	3	150	13
Out	35	2,921	
10	4	423	2
11	3	109	18
12	5	460	10
13	4	290	16
14	3	188	12
15	4	396	6
16	4	394	8
17	4	304	14
18	4	415	4
In	35	2,979	
Tot	70	5,900	

The 4th hole is a short (455 yards) par-5 that goes out to the ocean. The 5th hole is another beauty, a difficult 193-yard par-3 that is all uphill.

Meanwhile, the 16th is intriguing. A straightaway par-4 that measures just under 400 yards, this hole is made all the more interesting by its green that sits 10 feet below the fairway. Consequently, this is almost always a blind shot.

Wianno was the site of one of the better caddie camps in the 1930s. Many of the members helped campers with their college tuition later in life. Sometimes the members took care of the caddies' immediate needs.

"I'll always remember Mr. Kroger," says Joe Coughlin, who worked as a caddie in the early 1930s. "He was from the Midwest, a millionaire several times over. He owned the Kroger food stores. More than once he bought ice cream for the entire caddie camp."

10th HOLE *The Challenge*

Depending on the time of the year, this hole can be a killer.

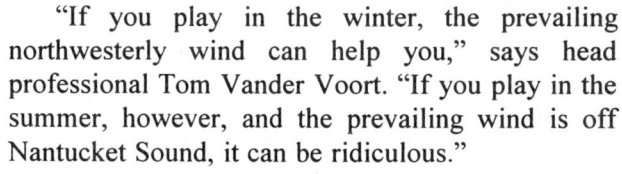

"If you play in the winter, the prevailing northwesterly wind can help you," says head professional Tom Vander Voort. "If you play in the summer, however, and the prevailing wind is off Nantucket Sound, it can be ridiculous."

Playing 423 yards from the members' tees, this is a straightaway par-4. The fairway rolls down, then back up, all of which helps make this hole is the most difficult on the back 9.

"You have to hit your drive to the top of the fairway," advises Vander Voort. "If you don't, you will have a blind second shot from a valley."

There is a fairway bunker at the bottom of the valley, and 3 more frame the green. The green is a good putting surface, but there is a lot of undulation from back-to-front.

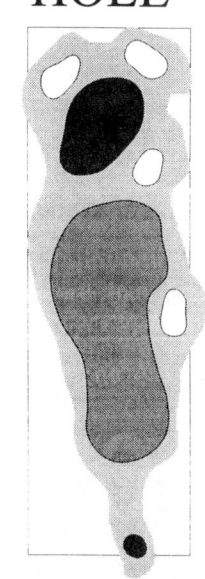

Willowbend

1988: Mashpee/477-8888

Architect: Michael Hurdzan
Course Rating: 73.0 **Course Slope:** 136
Course Record: 3-under 68 by Donnie Hammond
Tee Time Policy: Private course
Amenities: Motor carts, alcohol bar, food service
The Skinny: All this course needs is time and a major tournament.
Directions: From the Sagamore Bridge, take Route 6 east to Exit 2. From the ramp, turn right onto Route 130 south and follow this through Sandwich and Mashpee to its very end at Route 28 in Barnstable.
　Turn right onto Route 28. Follow this for a little more than a mile and watch on your left for Quinaquisset Avenue, which angles sharply back in the opposite direction. (Don't worry if you miss the road and suddenly arrive at the traffic circle; finding Quinaquisset might be easier coming back on Route 28.)
　Turn onto Quinaquisset Avenue and follow this winding road another mile or so. The Willowbend Club will be on your left.

The Course

Beginning as a wonderful project by Dick Hostetter and Bob St.Thomas, the history of The Willowbend Club has been nothing less than a rollercoaster ride.

Their dream was to make it a high-end private/residential community course, so Hostetter and St. Thomas hired architect Michael Hurdzan to build the golf course. He had just finished Dennis Highlands, the public course on Cape Cod.

Once the course was complete, house lots went on the market. But then the economy went into a tailspin. The Sentry Bank of Hyannis foreclosed on its loan just before federal regulators closed down the bank itself.

Fortunately, Reebok CEO Paul Fireman purchased the course in 1991, and Willowbend made a resurgence. Hurdzan returned to improve a few of the weaker holes on the back 9 and to create 3

Hol	Par	Yds	Hcp
1	5	526	9
2	3	197	13
3	4	374	11
4	4	395	7
5	3	160	17
6	4	430	1
7	3	154	15
8	5	546	5
9	4	447	3
Out	35	3,220	
10	5	530	12
11	4	435	6
12	4	417	8
13	3	160	18
14	4	402	10
15	4	402	4
16	3	188	16
17	4	419	2
18	5	495	14
In	36	3,565	
Tot	71	6,785	

entirely new ones to make a stronger course. He built a new, par-3 13th, and back-to-back par-4s for the 14th and 15th holes.

Still, many of Hurdzan's original holes are interesting to play. The 1st is an ideal starting hole, a testing par-5 with water fronting the green. The 3rd is a par-4 where you must decide whether to risk with the driver or else lay up. The 5th is a delightful par-3 over water from a horseshoe tee.

The abandoned, original 10th hole, a wonderful little par-3 with terrific mounding, still remains in front of the golf course, where they call in the 19th hole.

Every summer Fireman brings in some of the top players in the world, such as Greg Norman, John Daly and Brad Faxon, to test his course in a charity tournament. Willowbend also co-hosts the MGA's Mid-Amateur Championship with The Country Club of New Seabury every October.

There has been talk that some day Fireman will bring a professional tournament to Willowbend. That would make The Willowbend Club one of *the* premier courses in New England.

17th HOLE — *The Challenge*

"If this isn't *the* most challenging hole on Cape Cod," says assistant pro Chris Holmes, "it is the second most challenging." He's played every hole on Cape Cod, and the only one that compares is the 18th at Eastward Ho!, which *might* be better.

A par-4 dogleg right that's 419 yards from the members' tees, it is the toughest stroke hole on the back 9. You hit from an elevated tee, and the fairway runs into bunkers and a cranberry bog. You can hit anything from a driver to a 3-iron on this hole, but sometimes it is better to hit the 3-iron and hug it close to the hazard. That way can take a 2-iron or a 3-iron to run it up there. If you hit a driver too far, your second shot will be all carry.

There are 2 bunkers 50 yards in front of the left side of the green and another greenside. Just hope the pin is not on the back tier of the green, because that will only make the hole just that much harder.

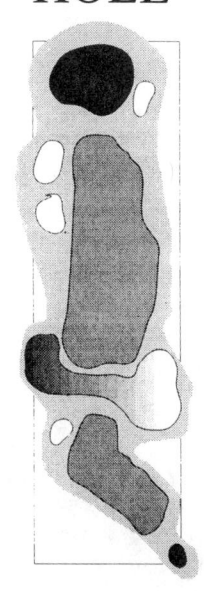

Woodbriar

1973: Falmouth/540-1600

Architect: William G. Robinson, Geoffrey Cornish
Course Rating: N/A **Course Slope:** N/A
Course Record: Unknown
Tee Time Policy: First come, first play
Amenities: Motor carts & pull carts, alcohol bar, food service
The Skinny: A *great* place for a beginner!
Directions: From the Bourne Bridge, take Route 28 all the way south to Falmouth, where 28 becomes Palmer Avenue. At the traffic light, (where your right turn is Ter Heun Drive to Falmouth Hospital), turn left onto Jones Road, then turn left at the next light onto Gifford Street. Woodbriar is along Gifford Street on the right.

The Course

When Geoffrey Cornish and William Robinson built this executive course in 1973, the 9-hole facility was called the Grasmere Golf Course, a part of the neighboring motel complex. In 1978, though, the Woodbriar Retirement Home purchased the motel and the golf course together.

"It isn't a difficult course," admits Ken Collins of Woodbriar. "So it's a good place for beginners and senior citizens."

Still, very few of the Woodbriar residents frequent the golf course. Probably because a good many them are over 85 years old.

There was, however, the late Anton Lee, who enjoyed playing these fairways and greens on sunny mornings right up until he died at the age of 103. In fact, notes Collins, Lee got his name and Woodbriar's into the *Guinness Book of Records* as the oldest golfer ever get a hole-in-one. On

Hol	Par	Yds	Hcp
1	3	142	9
2	3	129	15
3	3	115	17
4	3	139	11
5	3	230	1
6	3	162	5
7	3	168	3
8	3	127	13
9	3	158	7
Out	27	1,410	
10	3	142	10
11	3	129	16
12	3	115	18
13	3	139	12
14	3	230	2
15	3	162	6
16	3	168	4
17	3	127	14
18	3	158	8
In	27	1,410	
Tot	54	2,820	

September 24, 1982, Lee scored his ace on the 129-yard 2nd hole when he was 94 years, 9 months, and 24 days old, perhaps making him the oldest golfer to get an ace anywhere on Cape Cod, Nantucket & Martha's Vineyard. Since he died in 1991, a plaque at the golf course notes his accomplishment.

Meanwhile, the Hole-in-One Clearinghouse notes that the record is now held by an Otto Butcher of Geneva, Switzerland, who scored his ace at the age of 99.

As for the rest of us youngsters, be aware that water comes into play on 2 holes: the 168-yard 7th and the 158-yard 9th. The water, however, is not the factor that will send you muttering from the 9th hole. It is the slope of the green. You don't want a downhill putt.

5th HOLE

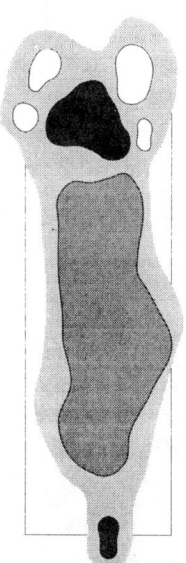

The Challenge

This 230-yard par-3 is a problem for every golfer.

Sure, scratch golfers can reach the green and sneak away with a par; however, the average player who cannot reach in regulation must be ready to think differently.

If you are not a long hitter, put yourself in position so you have a good chip to the pin on the green.

Don't skull your second shot over the green. There are 4 bunkers to catch your ball.

If the prevailing wind is blowing in your face, you are in for an ordeal.

Woods Hole

1899: Woods Hole/548-2932

Architect: Thomas Winton, (r) Wayne Stiles, John van Kleek
Course Rating: 69.7 **Course Slope:** 121
Course Record: 6-under 65 by Larry McDonald (1979), Joe Henley (1989)
Tee Time Policy: Private course
Amenities: Motor carts, alcohol bar, food service
The Skinny: Prepare for a lot of uneven lies.

Directions: From the Bourne Bridge, take Route 28 south the west end of Main Street in Falmouth, then follow Woods Hole Road south toward Woods Hole. At the traffic light, turn right onto Quissett Harbor Road. Turn left onto Quissett Avenue and continue 1 mile to Woods Hole on your right.

The Course

Incorporating in 1898, Woods Hole became one of the very first courses on Cape Cod, Nantucket & Martha's Vineyard when it opened for play the following year. The earliest course was 9 holes totaling 3,036 yards, and the original clubhouse was an oversized Cape Cod cottage near where the 11th tee sits today.

Of course, Woods Hole has the wind that blows constantly, but this is not your typical Cape & Islands golf course. The tees, the fairways, and the greens roll along like enormous waves so that there are *very* few flat lies.

In 1902, there were 22 full members and 17 associate members. Some 250 people played a little more than 2,800 rounds, and the club maintained that it needed another 20 members to ensure permanency of the club. So, the members placed an advertisement in the *Falmouth Enterprise*, but they

Hol	Par	Yds	Hcp
1	4	318	15
2	4	394	1
3	3	166	13
4	4	334	7
5	4	362	9
6	3	121	17
7	4	399	5
8	5	505	11
9	4	370	3
Out	35	2,969	
10	4	370	6
11	5	525	2
12	4	475	14
13	3	188	16
14	4	305	12
15	4	359	10
16	4	440	4
17	3	126	18
18	4	352	8
In	36	3,248	
Tot	71	6,117	

still had trouble filling their membership roles until 1909. By 1913, Woods Hole became a member of both the United States Golf Association and the Massachusetts Golf Association.

In 1916, it purchased the land on the northwest side of Quissett Avenue and hired Scot architect Thomas Winton to expand the course to 18 holes. When that was completed, Francis Ouimet established the course record of 72 in the inaugural round of 1919.

One of the only caddie strikes ever to take place at a golf course happened at Woods Hole in the 1920s. Caddies received 30 cents an hour, but they held out for 40 cents an hour and got it.

Shortly after that, George R. Faxon opened the Woods Hole Caddie Camp behind the 15th fairway in 1929.

Up until 1963, transient golfers could play Woods Hole, but since then guests can only play with members.

In the 1980s, Woods Hole member Gene McAuliffe, the 1960 Women's State Amateur champion, became the first woman in Massachusetts (if not the entire nation) to chair a club's important Greens Committee.

17th HOLE *The Challenge*

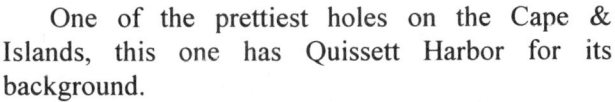

One of the prettiest holes on the Cape & Islands, this one has Quissett Harbor for its background.

You are hitting your drive from an elevated tee, 50 feet above the green, and the distance from the members tees is only 126 yards.

The green seems the size of a postage stamp with 6 bunkers around it, and you know that the wind whipping off Quissett Harbor will play tricks with your shot. That's just one aspect that makes this so challenging.

Another reason is the second-guessing of your club on the tee. With no more than a wedge in your hand, you still know it is too much. This is a feel shot. You can't take a club and swing away, knowing it will go the proper distance. Instead, you hit it as hard as you feel you must to reach the green.

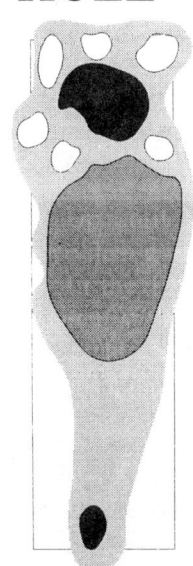

The Game of Golf
L. C. Hall
April, 1923

To the non-golfer, there is always something funny about this game. To see grown men and women walking about the landscape, clad in grotesque garments, swatting a little white ball, and getting excited about it always appeals to their sense of humor.

But to a golfer there is nothing funny about it. It's a serious business, and when one succeeds in lessening his score by a few strokes, he is as proud as though he had made a million dollars. He will tell you that proficiency in the game can only be acquired by long practice, and he will never admit that the element of luck enters into it at all — at least not in *his* game, though he may be ready to assert that his opponent is the possessor of a lucky rabbit's foot.

To call the game "cow pasture pool" is as deadly an insult as can be hurled at a genuine golfer, and to call it a game wherein one chases a white pill, who is too old too chase anything else, is adding injury to insult.

For, be it known, golf is a grand old game, hallowed by time, and indulged in by the most prominent people of this earth — and others. Most golfers will agree with Abe Martin "that the game of golf is needlessly prolonging the life of our most useless citizens," though they omit the words "needlessly" and "useless." They are enthusiastic in their claims for its health-giving qualities and are always ready to prescribe it as a cure-all for the ills to which men are prone, especially the tired business man. After all, the game of golf is capable of double enjoyment: once while it is being played, and forever afterward when it is being talked about.

One of the chief charms of both playing and talking golf is that it has a language all its own. The game is played on grounds called "links," which are studded with *greens, fairways, bunkers, traps,* and other *hazards,* dry and wet. Its chief implements are the *driver,* the *iron,* the *mashie,* the *niblick,* the *brassie,* the *jigger,* the *putter,* the *cleek,* and other variously crooked and potent instruments which are carried about by a *caddie.* The spectators constitute the *gallery.* These are but a few sample terms which the golfer employs, and the first requisite when learning to play is to dress and talk the part. Woe betide the duffer who calls a club out of its right name, for to do so proclaims him an amateur of the rankest type.

It is a libel to claim that golf is played only by old men. Young and old are to be found on the links on any pleasant day, and both sexes are sure to be represented. The seasoned golfer has a horror of being roped into a "mixed foursome," but the terrors of it are never sufficient to keep him at home.

Golf is great for the imagination, which it expends to an almost unbelievable degree. Some of the wild and wonderful tales heard in the clubhouse can be accounted for in no other way. It is also great in its cultivation of self-restraint. Even ministers of the gospel have to exercise it in a remarkable degree when they foozle a drive or top a mashie shot.

The game puts the player on his honor. There is no umpire or referee, and the player counts his own strokes, then puts down his own score, which his opponent is bound to accept as being true, both in statement and in fact. Any golfer in the rough, for example, who is seen to swing his club more numerously than his final score seems to account for, can always claim that he was killing a snake, and the explanation is bound to be accepted by all good and true golfers.

The chief charm of golf, though, is in the hopeful mind of the player. However hopeless his game, he *always* expects to do better.

Every game starts off with high hopes for breaking a record, and the fact of its non-accomplishment never totally discourages. The player who puts up a miserable appearance may seem discouraged, but it is never actually so. He may vow that he will never play another game as long as he lives, break up his clubs, and give his stock of balls to his caddie, but the next day *always* sees him back again with a new outfit and as hopeful as ever.

As a rule, men do not take up golf with premeditation. Instead, they are beguiled into it. After being induced to visit the links with a friend, they assume a supercilious air, then make a lot of scurrilous remarks, tell all the stale jokes, and in the usual manner try to impress the golfers that they are above playing such a child-like game. They intimate that they could play golf if they wanted to, and they express surprise that anyone should consider it difficult or attractive.

Meanwhile, the golfer listens patiently as long as he can before he *dares* the novice to try it. After considerable argument, a club is introduced into his hand, and a ball is teed up for his benefit. The novice takes a mighty swing, calculated to knock the ball far into the next county. Sometimes the stroke is successful, and the ball flies down the fairway toward the distant green and manly pride swells the bosom of the newly-made golfer. More often, however, the stroke is either a clean miss, or else the ball merely trickles a few feet before it comes to a rest. In either case, the deed has been done. A golfer has been born. If the results were good, he opines that he can do *even better* the next shot, and if his first shot has been unsuccessful his exasperation knows no bounds, and a determination takes possession of him to learn to play the game if it takes a week.

Few men were ever known to quit after a beginning had been made. The golf germ is insidious and persistent.

Seriously, golf has added greatly to the pleasures of this life and the healthfulness of a nation. Hours spent in the open air, the exercise of walking, the muscle building and the lung-filling, all are conducive to the renewal of bodily tissues.

But perhaps the greatest effect that golf has upon a man is the mental effect. No man ever played a good game of golf unless his mind was upon it. He must forget his worries and his cares and give himself up entirely to it. The fate of nations and corporations may depend upon him, but those things must wait while he plays his game of golf. His mind is clarified, and he is better enabled to solve his problems on account of the relaxation he has had.

That is why big thinkers like golf. It sweeps the cobwebs out of their brains and makes them better able to sleep and digest their food.

The nation little knows how much it has been indebted to golf. Were the fact better understood there would be fewer communities without links. Baseball must look to its laurels if it is to be continued as the great American game. So many people are playing golf nowadays that the non-golfer is looked upon with pity and is a subject for commiseration.

Golf is a vacation necessity. Without it, vacations would be useless. Take the case of the President of the United States; no sooner does Congress adjourn than he gathers up his golf sticks and departs for the Sunny South, where he travels from place to place, playing the game every day, forgetful of the neglect of Congress to pass the ship subsidy bill, to establish an international peace court, or to appropriate the money for the Cape Cod canal.

He is serenely happy while his brief vacation lasts, and every day the nation awaits breathlessly the news that he has broken his record and made a score of less than three figures. No golfer will criticize him for leaving the cold, fuel-less north at such a critical time, for they realize that golf is essential to his mental well-being, and that when he returns he will be better fitted to cope with and solve the great questions of state.

No golfer ever needs to recite the formula of Dr. Cone during the golf season, for every day, in every way they known that they are getting better and better, so long as they are able to get out to the links and their game continues to improve.

A man may be proud of his ancestry, proud of his achievements in science, art, literature, statesmanship, or business, but the real acme of his hopes is to *some* day, in *some* way, be able to say that he has been scratch man in a golf tournament.

— A —
Adams, Quincy Shaw 20
Andrade, Billy 55
American Junior Golf Association 53
Andrade, Billy 90
Ansewitz, Peter 75
ASHUMUTH VALLEY 43,97, 124

— B —
Babineau, Norm 67
Bacon, Dr. Gorham 18,78
Baker, Bob 67
Baker, Lorenzo Dow 72
Baldock, Robert 120
BALLYMEADE 48,49,50, 51,55,58-59
Baltusrol Golf Club 27
Barkhouse, Robert 66
Barmakian, Edd 112
BASS RIVER 18,45,51,54,60-61,62
BAYBERRY HILLS 51,62-63
Bay Hill 132
BAY POINTE 43,48,50,52,64-65
BEN LOMOND 20
Benson, Peter 110
Berg, Pat 66
Bigelow, Robert 112
Biles, Leonard 148
Birch, Charlie 84
Birds-eye Classic 97
Blakely, Don 92,93
BLUE ROCK 41,42,43,51,54,66-67,96
Boniface, John 132
Bourque, Ulysses 48
Bowen, Lynnie 88
Bowler, Richard 106
Bradley, Pat 67
Brady, Mike 140,141
Brae Burn Country Club 49
Bragdon, Russ 98
BREWSTER GREENS 44, 48,116
Brogna, Vincent 128
Bronson, Ray 31
Bulliard Farm 109
Bullock, Ed 102
Bump, Carl 107
Butcher, Otto 153
Buttner, Bill 54,127

— C —
caddie 29
caddie camp 29-35, 36
Callahan, John 120,121
Campbell, Andrew 137
Canal Classic 53
Cannon, Paul 85
Caouette, Fred 96
Cape Cod Amateur 53, 102
CAPE COD 19,26,27,68-69
Cape Cod Junior Championship 53
Cape Cod National Seashore Park 21,53,95
Cape Cod Open 53,99
Cape Cod Pro-Am League 53-54, 99
CAPTAINS 45,51,62,70-71,80,116
Caranci, Charlie 142
Caranci, Jane 142
Carey, Kevin 83
Carr, Steve 128,129
Carr, William 128,129
carts 32,36
Cavicchi, Tom 102
Cawley, Leonard 104
CEDAR BANK 20,21
Cestone, Michael 123
Chapman, Robert 86
Chase, Bob 130,131
Chasson, Mark 100
CHATHAM BARS INN 18,45,139
CHEQUESETT 19,53,72-73
CHILTON HALL 49
Clark, Ron 120
CLAUSEN 27,68
Clinton, President William 55,90, 91,113
Coffin, Robert 140,141
Cohasset Golf Club 36
Collins, Ken 152
conditioning 28
Congressional Country Club 68
Conklin, Harold 95
Converse, Geoff 124
Cooke, Alistair 94

Coolidge, Calvin 74
COONAMESSET 27,30,31,68
Cooper, Harry 54
Cornish, Geoffrey 41,42,43,44,51,
 62,64,66,71,76,90,96,97,98,
 99,116,117,130,144,146,152
Cotton, Henry 123
COTUIT HIGHGROUND 19,
 74-75
Coughlin, Joe 30,31
Country Club (Brookline) 40,49,
 51,84,115,117
Courville, Peter 70
CRANBERRY VALLEY 43,44,
 45,46,51,76-77
Crash of '29 19,21,24,29,47,51
Crawford 20
criteria for ratings 27,28
Crooked Stick Country Club 51
Cross, Richard 134
Crowley, Bob 69
CUMMAQUID 18,20,21,51,78-79
Curley, Governor James Michael
 31,32
Cusick, Fred 97

— D —
Daly, John 55,151
Daniel, Beth 67
Davies, Chris 101
Davis, Charles Henry 61
DeBettencourt, Doug 91
Denehy 126
DENNIS HIGHLANDS 45,51,
 80-81,82,111
DENNIS PINES 43,45,51,54,
 82-83,119
design balance 27
Devlin, Bruce 132
Didriksen, Babe 31
Dimaggio, Dom 55
Donald, William A. 60
Duarte, Antone 95
DUNFEY'S 144
Dye, P.B. 49
Dye, Peter 48-49,51,58

— E —
EASTWARD HO! 18,21,26,
 30,45,54,84-85
EDGARTOWN 18,86-87
Eisenhower, President Dwight D.
 (Ike) 37
El Conquistador 132
Emmet, Devereaux 27,68
Erickson, Leif 66
esthetics 28
executive course 42
Ezinicki, Bill 114

— F —
FALMOUTH 20,43,46,88-89
Falmouth Enterprise 154
FARM NECK 44,51,55,90-91
Fasick, Jon 101
Faxon, Brad 30,54,55,151
Faxon, George R. (Ray) 30,31,155
Fazio, Jim 50,58
FIDDLER'S GREEN 43,97,144
Finlay, Alex 100,140
Fireman, Paul 50,55,150
Flanagan, Mike 72
Flynn, William S. 104
FORGES FIELD 49
Forse, Ron 100
Fowler Family 74
Fowler, Herbert 17,21,27,84,85
Francis, Manny 128,129
Franklin Park Golf Course 25
Friel, Phil 69

— G —
Gaquin, James 54
Gaquin, Lois 54
Garfield, Dorothy Small 34,35
Garvin, Steve 112
Ghioto, Fred 144,145
glacier 22,23,51
Glenn, John 40
Golf Digest 27,28,71,76,80,144
Golf Magazine 27,28
Gordon, John 146,147
GRASMERE 152
Great Depression 20,21,31,41,42
greens (sand) 26
Grout, John 140
Guinness Book of Records 152
Guldahl, Ralph 54

Gunnarson, Bob 50,64
Gunnarson, Rusty 50,64,148

— H —
Haberl, Jay 82,83,119
Haberl, Michael 83,118,119
Hall, Walter 37
Hallet, Jim 54,62,70,78
Hallett, Ron 117
Hammond, Donnie 150
Hardy, Charles 138,139
Harney, Michael 124,125
Harney, Paul 124
Harney, Tim 125
Harrelson, Ken 58,144,145
Harrison, Patricia 50,58
Harrison, Steve 48-50,58-59
Harvard 30
HARWICHPORT 18,92-93
HEAD OF THE BAY 49
Heffernan, Paul 122
Heher, John 74-75
Henley, Joe 156
Herron, Mickey 118
Hewins, Ron 63
Hewins, Walter 45,60,61,62
HIGHLAND GOLF LINKS 18,21, 25,26,34,35,53,94-95,136
Hill, George 138
Hoagland, Bror 86
Hole-in-One Clearinghouse 153
HOLLY RIDGE 43,51,96-97
Holmes, Chris 151
Holmes, Chuck 68-69
Hood, Frederick C. 27,28,104,105
Hornblower Memorial Tournament 127
Hostetter, Dick 150
Hurdzan, Dr. Michael 51,80,111, 150,151
Hutchinson, Bill 32
HYANNIS 44,51,53,98-99
HYANNISPORT 18,24,26,29,31-34,36-40,43,48,49,53,78,96

— I —
ISLAND GOLF LINKS 44
Iwazsko, Richard 120
IYANOUGH HILLS 43,98

— J —
Jones, Bobby 17,21,34
Jones, Rees 49,51,114,115
Jones, Robert Trent 51,104

— K —
Keller, Joe 123,130
Kennedy, Ethel 40
Kennedy, Jacqueline 38,39
Kennedy, President John F. 20,29, 32,36-40,96
Kennedy, Joseph P. 36,37
Kennedy, Patricia 33
Kennedy, Robert F. 40,55
kettles 22
King, Betsy 55,67
KINGS WAY 51,102-103
Kirby, Ed 82,118
KITTANSETT 19,27,28,55,83, 104-105

— L —
LaCava, Tony 130
Ladies Professional Golf Association (LPGA) 24,54
Lawford, Peter 33-34
Lawrence, Dean 97
Leary, Leona 44-45
Lee, Anton 152
Lewis, Jeff 68,78
Lewis, Keith 80
Lind, Jenny 95
links 23
LITTLE HARBOR 42,51,52,106-107
LITTLE MARION 27,108-109
Litten, Karl 146
Lizotte, Peter 145
Long Cove 51
Lyons, John 135

— M —
Madson, Craig 83
Mann, Michael 106,107
Marble, Ralph 110
Marchant Farm 106
Marion (*see* Little Marion)
Marr, Dave 48,66
Martin, Tom 67

Mason-Dixon line 24
Massachusetts Golf Association
 (MGA) 24,74,83,101,122
Masters Tournament 54,127
Maxwell, General Robert 39
McAuliffe, Gene 155
McBroom, Mike 118
McCarthy, Daniel 96
McCarthy, Gene 43
McDonald, Larry 154
McHale, Kevin 48
McKinley, J. Henry 26,94
McNamara, Robert S. 39
McSpaden, Harold 123
Medeiros, Bill 110
Mello, Ray 66
Mellon Family 122
memorability 27
MENAUHANT 20
Merion Cricket Club 27,109
MIACOMET 42,110-111
Miller, Bob 66,67
Milligan, Peter 90
MINK MEADOWS 20,29,112-113
Mitchell, Henry 51,78,79,82,120
Mitchell, Robert 51
Mitchell, Sam 51,106,107
Mitchell, William 51,114,115
Moon Valley 132
Moore, Sherwood A. 73
moors 23
moraines 22,23,25,43
Morgan, Peter 76,136
Morrison, George 53-54
Morse, Andy 114,130
Mungeam, Mark 118
Murphy, Bruce 118,134,142

— N —
NANTUCKET GOLF LINKS 18, 26
National Golf Links 27
Nelson, Byron 54
New England Professional Golf
 Association (NE PGA) 48, 116,117,136
NEW SEABURY (The Country
 Club of) 43,47,51,53,88, 114-115,125,151
Niblet, Tom 36-40,43,49,96,97,133
Nickerson, George 60
Norman, Greg 55,151
North Hill Country Club 50
Norton Country Club 43

— O —
OAK BLUFFS 18,88
OCEAN EDGE 48,49,51,62, 118-119
O'Hearn, Brian 64
Ohlson, Alex 43
OLDE BARNSTABLE
 FAIRGROUNDS 46, 51, 99, 118-119
Oliver, Ed 69
OTIS 42,43,120-121
Ouimet, Francis 17,21,67,85, 94,114,123,155
outwash 22,23
OYSTER HARBORS 19,26,29, 30,31,49,122-123

— P —
Paganis, Tony 128,129
Paine, Frederick 26,100
Palmer, Arnold (Golf Management
 Company) 59
Parente, Robert 104
Park, Willie 27
PAUL HARNEY 43,97,124-125
Pease Farm, Captain Chase 86
Pebble Beach Golf Club 48
Perez, Louis 48
Philbrick, Gary 118,119
Phillips, Otis 64
Picard, Henry 54,127
Pilgrims 19,22
Pine Brook 49
Pine Valley Golf Club 27,97,109
Pitts, Fordie 98
Player, Gary 47,51,146,147
Pleasant Valley Country Club
 73,125
PLYMOUTH 18,26,54, 126-127
POCASSET 18,26,120,128-129
Pollard, Allan 92
Porkka, Dave 98,99

Professional Golfers Association
    (PGA) 54
Prophett, Bob 128
Pry, Mike 115

— Q —
QUASHNET VALLEY 44,51,
    130-131
Quinlan, Sally 54,67

— R —
Rabesa, Lou 88
Reed, John 18,78
resistance to scoring 27
Rezendes, Joe 108
Rezendes, Susan 108
Richard, Ray, Jr. 142
RIDGE CLUB 49,51,97,132-133
Riley, James 32,33
Robinson, William G. 66,76,98,
    130,152
Rodriguez, Chi Chi 50,55,58
Ross, David 123
Ross, Donald 17,18,21,26,27,60,
    61,68,100,109,122,126,127,
    128,136,148
Ross Society 26
ROUND HILL 43,53,134-136
Royal St. George Golf Links 26
Ruschioni, Jim 130

— S —
Sances, Jack 78,98,120
St. Andrew's (Hyannisport) 31
St. Andrew's (New York) 18,78
St. Andrew's (Scotland) 86,104
St. Thomas, Bob 27,48,50,150
Salinger, Pierre 39
SANKATY HEAD LINKS 19,28,
    29,34,136-137
SANTUIT 20
Sarazen, Gene 54,123
Savery, Ed 74
Scotland 23
Seagulls Tournament 53,101
SEAPUIT 18,20
SEASIDE LINKS 46,138-139
Shea, Tom 105
Shepard, James 62
shot value 27

SIASCONSET 18,140-141
Silva, Brian 44,51,58,62,63,64,90,
    102,116,117,118
Silva, David 94
Simonelli, Peter 59
SIPPEWISSET 20
Sjorgen, Dick 73
Small, Isaac Morton 25,34,94
Small, Willard 25,94
Smith, Horton 54,123
soil 23
Souza, Tony 75
Spalding, Charles (Chuck) 39,40
Sports Illustrated 67,95,107
Spring, Tim 113
SQUIRREL RUN 142-143
Stackpole, Charlie 110-111
Stewart, Brian 78
Stewart, Paul 34
Stiles, Wayne 20,89,154
Stimets, Dick 123
Striar, Soozen 135
Surette, Mark 103

— T —
Taylor, John I. 128
TARA WOODS 43,51,97,
    144-145
tees (sand) 25,26,30
Tedesco, Guy 88
Tellier, Louis 141
Thacher, Henry 18,78
Thomas, George C. 27,108-109
Thoren, John 69
Tillinghast, A.W. 27,109,136
Tournament Players Club 132
TPC Woodlands 132
TREADWAY 27,68
Tucker Anthony Classic 53,97,133
Tull, Alfred 27,68
TUPANCY 20
Turner, Ted 148

— U —
United Kingdom 21
United States Golf Association
    (USGA) 54,74,83,84,123
US Open 21,40,49,51,115
Uva, Louis 107

— V —

Van Cortland Golf Club 25
Vanderhoop, Lynn 112
Vander Voort, Tom 149
van Kleek, John 20,89,154
Vikings 22
Volpe, Sam 134
von Hagge, Robert 49,51,132

— W —

Wachusett Country Club 88
Walker Cup 24,28,104
Walton Heath 84
Wampanoags 22,130
WAREHAM 48,64
Wee Burn Country Club 68
Wessner, Tom 112
Westward Ho! 21,84
WHITE CLIFFS 47,49,51,146-147
Whillock, Steve 116,117
WIANNO 18,26,30,31,32, 148-149
Wild Dunes 59
WILLOWBEND 20,48,50,51, 55, 80,111,150-151
Wilson, Dick 134
Wilson, Hugh 108
Windeler, G. Herbert 84
Winged Foot Golf Club 27,73
Winton, Thomas 27,154
Wodehouse, P.G. 20
Wogan, Phil 130
Wogan, Skip 136
Wood, Carri 54, 67
WOODBRIAR 43,51, 152-153
WOODS HOLE 18, 27, 30, 31, 54, 154-155

— Y —

Yale College 25

— Z —

Zoll, Mike 90

Bibliography

Armstrong, H. Emerson. "Nantucket Island from a Golfing Standpoint." *CAPE COD and All the Pilgrim Land*, March 1922.

Edward Bullock. *Cape Cod Golf Guide.* On-Cape Lithographers (Harwich Port, MA: 1986)

Cook, Norman H. "Economics" in *The Seven Villages of Barnstable.* Town of Barnstable (Barnstable, MA: 1976)

Cornish, Geoffrey S., and Whitten, Ronald E. *The Architects of Golf.* Harper and Collins (New York: 1993)

Crane, Mary Hinckley. "Barnstable," in *The Seven Villages of Barnstable*, Town of Barnstable (Barnstable, MA: 1976)

Frederick, William. "Bass River Suits Average Golfer." *Cape Cod Magazine and Cape Cod Life*, July 11, 1927.

--------. "New Golf Course at Falmouth." *Cape Cod Magazine and Cape Cod Life*, April/May 1928.

--------. "How Donald Ross Manufactured A Golf Course." *Cape Cod Magazine*, March 15, 1927.

--------. "Where 10,000 Tee Off in a Season." *Cape Cod Magazine and Cape Cod Life*, August 1, 1927.

Goodwin, Doris Kearns. *The Fitzgeralds and the Kennedys.* Simon & Schuster (New York: 1987)

Hall, L.C. "Golf on the Cape." *Cape Cod Magazine*, January/February 1924.

Lipsey, Rick. "Caddie Camps: A colorful part of golf history on the verge of extinction." *Golf Illustrated*, April 1991.

Lowenthal, Larry. "The Truro Family, 1879-1932." *Cape Cod Life*, August/September 1993.

Mahoney, Jack. *The History of New England Golf.* Wellesley Press, Inc. (Framingham, MA: 1973).

Moriarty, Jim. "Where Golf's Pilgrims Gather." *Golf Digest*, August 1987.

Silva, Brian, "Donald Ross, Dean of American Golf Course Architects." *US Golf Journal*, August 1986.

Sugerman, Michael, and Ablin, Jack. *New England Golf Guide.* GolfGuide Publications (Brookline, MA: 1993).

Wade, Don. "Perfect Place For Golf." *Golf Digest*, June 1991.

-------. "Island Golf with a Yankee Accent." *Golf Digest*, July 1993.

Whitten, Ronald. "The Best New Courses of the Year." *Golf Digest*, February 1986.

The Complete Guide to Golf on Cape Cod, Nantucket & Martha's Vineyard

This book could not have been completed without the help of so many persons. Special thanks to Don Davidson, whose idea it was to create this book.

Many thanks also to Christine Buckley, Ed Bullock, John Callahan, Paul Cannon, Geoff Cornish, Geoff Converse, Joe Coughlin, Chris Davies, Gardner Drew, Dan Duarte, Jim and Lois Gaquin, Brad Graber, Fred Ghioto, Mickey Herron, Mark Hess, Rich Iwaszko, Leona Leary, Manny Macara, Tom Niblet, Gary Philbrick, May Pollard, Sue Rezendez, Jim Riley, Ed Semprini, Dick Sjorgen, and Tim Spring.

P.H.